In Light of India

OCTAVIO PAZ

In Light of India

Translated from the Spanish by
Eliot Weinberger

A Harvest Book
Harcourt Brace & Company
SAN DIEGO   NEW YORK   LONDON

This is a translation of *Vislumbres de la India*.

"The Hymn of Creation" from *The Wonder that was India* by
A.L. Basham, © 1954 by Sidgwick & Jackson.
Reprinted by permission of the publisher.
Excerpt from "Sweeney Agonistes: Fragment of an Agon"
in *Collected Poems 1909-1962* by T.S. Eliot, copyright 1936
by Harcourt Brace & Company, © 1964, 1963 by T.S. Eliot,
reprinted by permission of the publisher.
Excerpts from *The Hermit and the Love Thief*, translated by Barbara
Stoler Miller. Copyright © 1978 by Columbia University Press.
Reprinted with permission of the publisher.

Library of Congress Cataloging-in-Publication Data
Paz, Octavio, 1914–
[Vislumbres de la India. English]
In light of India: essays/Octavio Paz; translated from the
Spanish by Eliot Weinberger.—1st ed.
p.   cm.
Includes bibliographical references.
ISBN 0-15-100222-3
ISBN 0-15-600578-6 (pbk.)
1. India—Civilization. 2. Paz, Octavio, 1914–
3. Ambassadors—Mexico—Travel. 4. Ambassadors—India—Travel.
5. Authors, Mexican—Journeys—India. I. Weinberger, Eliot.
II. Title.
DS423.P4313   1997
954—dc21   96-45756   CIP

Text set in Bembo
Designed by Lori McThomas Buley
Printed in the United States of America
First Harvest edition 1998
A C E D B

CONTENTS

CONTENTS

In Light of India

The Antipodes
of Coming and Going

... in order not to fall into the Errors of the
ancient Philosophers, who believed that there
are no Antipodes.

—FATHER ALONSO DE OVALLE,
Diccionario de Autoridades

BOMBAY

In 1951 I was living in Paris. I had a modest job at the Mexican Embassy, having arrived six years earlier, in December 1945. The mediocrity of my position perhaps explains why, after two or three years, I had not been transferred to another post, as is the diplomatic custom. My superiors had forgotten me, and I secretly thanked them. I was trying to write and, most of all, I was exploring the city that is probably the most beautiful example of the genius of our civilization: solid without heaviness, huge without gigantism, tied to the earth but with a desire for flight. A city where moderation rules the excesses of both the body and the head with the same gentle and unyielding authority. In its most auspicious moments—a square, an avenue, a group of buildings—tension turns to harmony, a pleasure for the eyes and for the mind. Exploration and recognition: in my walks and rambles I discovered new places and neighborhoods, but there were others that I recognized, not by sight but from novels and poems. Paris for me is a city that, more than invented, is reconstructed by memory and the imagination. I saw a few friends, French and foreign, sometimes in their apartments, but usually in the cafés and bars. In Paris, as in other Latin cities, one lives more in the streets than at home. I met with friends with whom I shared artistic and intellectual affinities, and was immersed in the literary life of those days, with its clamorous philosophical and political debates. But my secret obsession was poetry: to write it, think it, live it. Excited by so many contradictory thoughts, feelings, and emotions, I was living each moment so intensely that it never occurred to me that this way of life would ever change. The future—that is, the unexpected—had almost completely evaporated.

One day the Ambassador called me to his office and, without saying a word, handed me a cable: I had been transferred. The news was bewildering and painful. It was normal that I should be sent elsewhere, but I was devastated to leave Paris. The reason for my transfer was that the government of Mexico had formally established relations with India, which had gained its independence in 1947, and now was planning to open a mission in Delhi. Knowing that I was being sent to India consoled me a little: rituals, temples, cities whose names evoked strange tales, motley and multicolored crowds, women with feline grace and dark and shining eyes, saints, beggars. . . . That same morning I learned that the person who had been named ambassador was Emilio Portes Gil, a well-known and influential man who had once been the President of Mexico. Besides the Ambassador, the staff would consist of a consul, an under-secretary (myself), and two counselors.

Why had they chosen me? No one told me, and I never would learn the reason. But there were rumors that my transfer had come at the suggestion of the poet Jaime Torres Bodet, then Director General of UNESCO, to Manuel Tello, the Minister of Foreign Affairs. It seemed that Torres Bodet was disturbed by some of my literary activities, and had been particularly displeased by my participation, with Albert Camus and María Casares, in an event commemorating the anniversary of the beginning of the Spanish Civil War (July 18, 1936), and organized by a group that was close to the Spanish anarchists. Although the Mexican government did not have relations with Franco—quite the opposite: it was the only country in the world that had an official ambassador to the Spanish Republic in Exile—Torres Bodet thought that my presence at that political-cultural gathering, and some of the things I said there, were "improper." I will never know if this story is true, but years later, at a dinner, I heard Torres Bodet make a curious confession. Talking about writers who had served in the diplomatic corps—Alfonso Reyes and José Gorostiza in Mexico, Paul Claudel and Saint-John Perse in France, among others—he added, "But one must avoid, at all costs, having two writers in the same embassy."

I said good-bye to my friends. Henri Michaux gave me a little anthology of poems by Kabīr, Krishna Riboud a print of the goddess Durga, and Kostas Papaioannou a copy of the *Bhagavad-Gītā*, which became my spiritual guide to the world of India. In the middle of my preparations, I received a letter from Mexico with instructions from the new Ambassador: I was to meet him in Cairo. With the rest of the staff, we would continue on to Port Said, where we would board a Polish ship, the *Batory*, that would take us to Bombay. The news was strange—normally we would have flown directly to Delhi—but I was delighted. It would give me a glimpse of Cairo, its museums and pyramids, and I would cross the Red Sea and see Aden before reaching Bombay.

When we arrived in Cairo, Portes Gil told us that he had changed his mind and would fly to Delhi. Later I realized that he had simply wanted to visit some places in Egypt before taking the plane to India. But in my case it was too late to change the plans: the steamship company couldn't refund my ticket quickly, and I didn't have the money for the plane. I decided to go by ship. Those were the last days of the reign of King Farouk and there were many riots—the famous Shepherd's Hotel was burned down soon after. The road from Cairo to Port Said was blocked at various points and considered unsafe. With two other passengers, I traveled in a car flying the Polish flag and, perhaps thanks to it, we arrived without incident.

The *Batory* was a German ship given to Poland as part of the war reparations. The crossing was pleasant, although the monotony of the passage across the Red Sea was at times oppressive: to the left and right, arid and barely undulating hills stretched out; the sea was grayish and calm. I thought: Nature too can be boring. The arrival in Aden broke the monotony. A picturesque highway through great rocks led from the port to the city. I wandered enchanted through the noisy bazaars, full of Levantines, Chinese, and Indians, and the neighboring streets and alleyways. The colorful crowds, the veiled women with eyes as deep as the water in a well, the faces of the passers-by as anonymous as those in any city, but dressed in oriental clothes; beggars, busy people, groups talking loudly, laughter, and, amid the throng, silent Arabs with noble features and a forbidding demeanor. Hanging from their belts, an empty sheath for a knife or dagger. They were desert people who had to give up their weapons before entering the city. Only in Afghanistan have I seen a people with similar grace and dignity.

Life on board the *Batory* was lively, the group heterogeneous. The strangest passenger was a maharajah with a monastic face, who was surrounded by obsequious servants. Due to some ritual vow, he avoided all contact with foreigners, and in the dining room his chair had ropes around it to keep the other passengers from coming too close. Also on board was an elderly woman who was the widow of the sculptor Brancusi; she'd been invited to India by a magnate who admired her husband. There was a group of nuns, most of them Polish, who prayed every morning at five in a mass officiated by two Polish priests. They were on their way to Madras, to a convent founded by their order. Although the Communists had taken power in Poland, the authorities on the ship pretended not to notice these religious activities, or perhaps their tolerance was part of governmental policy at the time. It was moving to hear the mass sung by those nuns and priests on the morning we arrived in Bombay. Before us rose the coast of an immense and strange country populated by millions of infidels, some of whom worshiped masculine and feminine idols with powerful bodies or animal features, and others who prayed to the faceless God of Islam. I did not dare to ask them if they realized that their arrival in India was a late episode in the great failure of Christianity in these lands.... A couple who immediately attracted my attention were a pretty young Hindu woman and her husband, a young American. We quickly fell into conversation, and by the end of the voyage were good friends. She was Santha Rama Rau, the well-known writer and author of two notable adaptations, for the theater and for film, of *Passage to India*. He was Faubian Bowers, who had been an aide-de-camp to General MacArthur and was the author of a book on the Japanese kabuki theater.

We arrived in Bombay on an early morning in November 1951. I remember the intensity of the light despite the early hour, and my impatience at the sluggishness with which the boat crossed the quiet bay. An enormous mass of liquid mercury, barely undulating; vague hills in the distance; flocks of birds; a pale sky and scraps of pink clouds. As the boat moved forward, the excitement of the passengers grew. Little by little the white-and-blue architecture of the city sprouted up, a stream of smoke from a chimney, the ocher and green stains of a distant garden. An arch of stone appeared, planted on a dock and crowned with four little towers in the shape of pine trees. Someone leaning on the railing beside me exclaimed, "The Gateway of India!" He was an Englishman, a geologist bound for Calcutta. We had met two days before, and I had discovered that he was W. H. Auden's brother. He explained that the arch was a monument erected to commemorate the visit of King George V and his wife, Queen Mary, in 1911. It seemed to me a fantasy version of the Roman arches; later I learned it was inspired by an architectural style that had flourished in Gujarat, an Indian state, in the sixteenth century. Behind the monument, floating in the warm air, was the silhouette of the Taj Mahal Hotel, an enormous cake, a delirium of the fin-de-siècle Orient fallen like a gigantic bubble, not of soap but of stone, on Bombay's lap. I rubbed my eyes: was the hotel getting closer or farther away? Seeing my surprise, Auden explained to me that the hotel's strange appearance was due to a mistake: the builders could not read the plans that the architect had sent from Paris, and they built it backward, its front facing the city, its back turned to the sea. The mistake seemed to me a deliberate one that revealed an unconscious negation of Europe and the desire to confine the building forever in India. A symbolic gesture, much like that of Cortés burning the boats so that his men could not leave. How often have we experienced similar temptations?

Once on land, surrounded by crowds shouting at us in

English and various native languages, we walked fifty meters along the filthy dock and entered the ramshackle customs building, an enormous shed. The heat was unbearable and the chaos indescribable. I found, not easily, my few pieces of luggage, and subjected myself to a tedious interrogation by a customs official. Free at last, I left the building and found myself on the street, in the middle of an uproar of porters, guides, and drivers. I managed to find a taxi, and it took me on a crazed drive to my hotel, the Taj Mahal.

If this book were a memoir and not an essay, I would devote pages to that hotel. It is real and chimerical, ostentatious and comfortable, vulgar and sublime. It is the English dream of India at the beginning of the century, an India populated by dark men with pointed mustaches and scimitars at their waists, by women with amber-colored skin, hair and eyebrows as black as crows' wings, and the huge eyes of lionesses in heat. Its elaborately ornamented archways, its unexpected nooks, its patios, terraces, and gardens are both enchanting and dizzying. It is a literary architecture, a serialized novel. Its passageways are the corridors of a lavish, sinister, and endless dream. A setting for a sentimental tale or a chronicle of depravity. But that Taj Mahal no longer exists: it has been modernized and degraded, as though it were a motel for tourists from the Midwest. . . . A bellboy in a turban and an immaculate white jacket took me to my room. It was tiny but agreeable. I put my things in the closet, bathed quickly, and put on a white shirt. I ran down the stairs and plunged into the streets. There, awaiting me, was an unimagined reality:

waves of heat; huge grey and red buildings, a Victorian London growing among palm trees and banyans like a recurrent nightmare, leprous walls, wide and beautiful avenues, huge unfamiliar trees, stinking alleyways,

torrents of cars, people coming and going, skeletal cows with no owners, beggars, creaking carts drawn by enervated oxen, rivers of bicycles,

a survivor of the British Raj, in a meticulous and threadbare white suit, with a black umbrella,

another beggar, four half-naked would-be saints daubed with paint, red betel stains on the sidewalk,

horn battles between a taxi and a dusty bus, more bicycles, more cows, another half-naked saint,

turning the corner, the apparition of a girl like a half-opened flower,

gusts of stench, decomposing matter, whiffs of pure and fresh perfumes,

stalls selling coconuts and slices of pineapple, ragged vagrants with no job and no luck, a gang of adolescents like an escaping herd of deer,

women in red, blue, yellow, deliriously colored saris, some solar, some nocturnal, dark-haired women with bracelets on their ankles and sandals made not for the burning asphalt but for fields,

public gardens overwhelmed by the heat, monkeys in the cornices of the buildings, shit and jasmine, homeless boys,

a banyan, image of the rain as the cactus is the emblem of aridity, and, leaning against a wall, a stone daubed with red paint, at its feet a few faded flowers: the silhouette of the monkey god,

the laughter of a young girl, slender as a lily stalk, a leper sitting under the statue of an eminent Parsi,

in the doorway of a shack, watching everyone with indifference, an old man with a noble face,

a magnificent eucalyptus in the desolation of a garbage dump, an enormous billboard in an empty lot with a picture of a movie star: full moon over the sultan's terrace,

more decrepit walls, whitewashed walls covered with political slogans written in red and black letters I couldn't read,

the gold and black grillwork of a luxurious villa with a contemptuous inscription: EASY MONEY; more grilles even more luxurious, which allowed a glimpse of an exuberant garden; on the door, an inscription in gold on the black marble,

in the violently blue sky, in zigzags or in circles, the flights of seagulls or vultures, crows, crows, crows...

As night fell, I returned to my hotel, exhausted. I had dinner in my room, but my curiosity was greater than my fatigue: after another bath, I went out again into the city. I found many white bundles lying on the sidewalks: men and women who had no home. I took a taxi and drove through deserted districts and lively neighborhoods, streets animated by the twin fevers of vice and money. I saw monsters and was blinded by flashes of beauty. I strolled through infamous alleyways and stared at the bordellos and little shops: painted prostitutes and transvestites with glass beads and loud skirts. I wandered toward Malabar Hill and its serene gardens. I walked down a quiet street to its end and found a dizzying vision: there, below, the black sea beat against the rocks of the coast and covered them with a rippling shawl of foam. I took another taxi back to my hotel, but I did not go in. The night lured me on, and I decided to take another walk along the great avenue that ran beside the docks. It was a zone of calm. In the sky the stars burned silently. I sat at the foot of a huge tree, a statue of the night, and tried to make an inventory of all I had seen, heard, smelled, and felt: dizziness, horror, stupor, astonishment, joy, enthusiasm, nausea, inescapable attraction. What had attracted me? It was difficult to say: *Human kind cannot bear much reality*. Yes, the excess of reality had become an unreality, but that unreality had turned suddenly into a balcony from which I peered into—what? Into that which is beyond and still has no name...

In retrospect, my immediate fascination doesn't strike me as strange: in those days I was a young barbarian poet. Youth, poetry, and barbarism are not opposed to one another: in the gaze of a barbarian there is innocence; in that of a young man, an appetite for life; and in a poet's gaze, astonishment. The next day I called Santha and Faubian. They invited me for a drink at their house. They were living with Santha's parents in an elegant mansion that, like the others in Bombay, was surrounded by a garden. We sat on the terrace, around a table with refreshments. Soon after, her father joined us, a courtly man who had been the first Indian ambassador to Washington and had recently left his post. On hearing my nationality, he burst out laughing and asked: "And is Mexico one of the stars or one of the stripes?" I turned red and was about to answer rudely, when Santha intervened with a smile: "Forgive us, Octavio. The Europeans know nothing of geography, and we know nothing of history." Her father apologized. "It was only a joke.... We too, not so long ago, were also a colony." I thought of my compatriots: they say similar nonsense when talking about India. Santha and Faubian asked me if I had visited any of the famous sites. They told me to go to the museum and, above all, to visit the island of Elephanta.

The next day I went back to the dock and bought a ticket for the small boat that runs between Bombay and Elephanta. With me were various foreign tourists and a few Indians. The sea was calm; we crossed the bay under a cloudless sky and arrived at the small island in less than an hour. Tall white cliffs, and a rich and startling vegetation. We walked up a gray and red path that led to the mouth of an enormous cave, and I entered a world made of shadows and sudden brightness. The play of the light, the vastness of the space and its irregular form, the figures carved on the walls: all of it gave the place a sacred character, sacred in the deepest meaning of the word. In the shadows were the powerful reliefs and statues, many of them mutilated by the fanaticism of the Portuguese and the Muslims, but all of them majestic, solid, made of a solar material. Corporeal beauty, turned into living stone. Divinities of the earth, sexual incarnations of the most abstract thought, gods that were simultaneously intellectual and carnal, terrible and peaceful. Shiva smiles from a beyond where time is a small drifting cloud, and that cloud soon turns into a stream of water, and the stream into a slender maiden who is spring itself: the goddess Pārvatī. The divine couple are the image of a happiness that our mortal condition grants us only for a moment before it vanishes. That palpable, tangible, eternal

world is not for us. A vision of a happiness that is both terrestrial and unreachable. This was my initiation into the art
of India.

DELHI

A week later I took the train for Delhi. I didn't take a camera
with me, but I took a trusty guide: *Murray's Handbook of India,
Pakistan, Burma, and Ceylon*, in the 1949 edition, purchased
the day before in the bookstall of the Taj Mahal. On the first
page were three lines by Milton:

> India and the Golden Chersonese
> And utmost Indian Isle Taprobane,
> Dusk faces with white silken turbans wreathed.

That interminable journey, with its stations full of people
and the vendors of trinkets and sweets, made me think not of
the visions of an English poet of the seventeenth century, but
of some lines from a Mexican in the twentieth, Ramón López
Velarde:

> My country: your house is still
> so vast that the train going by
> seems like a Christmas box from a toyshop.

It was impossible not to recall another long train ride, as
desolate and with the same monotony which is one of the
attributes of immensity, that I took as a child with my mother
from Mexico City to San Antonio, Texas. It was near the end
of the Mexican Revolution, and we had a military escort on

board to protect us from the insurgents who were attacking the trains. My mother was suspicious of the officials: we were going to join my father, a political exile in the United States and the enemy of these military men. She was haunted by the hanged men she had seen on trips from Mexico City to Puebla, swaying from the telegraph poles along the way, their tongues dangling. Whenever we reached a station where the rebels had recently been fighting the federal troops, she would cover my face with one hand and with the other quickly lower the blinds on the window. I would be sleeping, and her gesture would make me open my eyes: once I saw an elongated shadow hanging from a pole. It was a brief glimpse, and before I could realize what it was, it vanished. I was six years old then. Remembering that incident as I watched the interminable plains of India, I thought of the massacres of Hindus and Muslims in 1947. Massacres along the railroad tracks, the same in India as in Mexico . . . From the beginning, everything that I saw inadvertently evoked forgotten images of Mexico. The strangeness of India brought to mind that other strangeness: my own country. The lines of Milton with their exoticism blended into my own familiar exoticism of being Mexican. I had just written *The Labyrinth of Solitude*, an attempt to answer the question that Mexico asked me; now India was asking another question, one that was far more vast and enigmatic.

In New Delhi, I settled in a small and pleasant hotel. New Delhi is unreal, like the Gothic architecture of nineteenth-century London or the Babylon of Cecil B. DeMille. That is to say, it is an assemblage of images more than buildings. Its aesthetic equivalent is to be found in novels, not in architecture: wandering the city is like passing through the pages of Victor Hugo, Walter Scott, or Alexandre Dumas. The period and the story are different, but the enchantment is the same. New Delhi was not built slowly over the centuries, reflecting the inspirations of successive generations. Like Washington, it was planned and constructed in a few years by a single architect: Sir Edwin Luytens. Despite the eclecticism of the style —a picturesque fusion of classical European and Indian architectures—the result is not only attractive but often sensational. The great marble masses of the old Viceroy's House, now the residence (Rashtrapati Bhavan) of the President of the Republic, has a grandeur to it. Its perfect Mughal-style gardens make one think of a giant chessboard on which each piece is a group of trees or a fountain. There are other notable buildings in the same hybrid style. The design of the city is harmonious: wide avenues with lines of trees, circular plazas, and a multitude of trees. New Delhi was conceived as a garden city. I was shocked, at my last visit in 1985, at its deterioration. The excessive growth of the population, the traffic with its smog, and the new districts built with cheap materials in a vulgar style had made New Delhi ugly. In certain parts, however, some beautiful new buildings had been built: among them, the American Embassy, and the smaller, lesser known Belgian Embassy, the imaginative creation of Satish Gujrat, a notable painter turned architect, who had been inspired by the architecture of Tughlakabad, whose grand and severe fourteenth-century ruins can be seen on the outskirts of Delhi.

New Delhi is the most recent of a series of cities built in the same area. The most ancient, from which nothing remains, was called Indrapashta, according to the epic poem the *Mahābhārata*. It is said to have flourished 1500 years before Christ. The city that preceded New Delhi was the work of the emperor Shah Jahān, the grandson of Akbar and the builder of the Taj Mahal. Old Delhi, as they now call Shah

Jahān's city, although destroyed by its masses of inhabitants and its poverty, contains beautiful buildings sadly maltreated by negligence and time. Its streets and alleyways, teeming with everyday life, are what the great cities of the Orient must have been like in the seventeenth and eighteenth centuries, as they are described in the chronicles of European travelers. The Red Fort, on the bank of the wide Jamuna River, is as powerful as a fort and as graceful as a palace. In its huge rooms, its gardens, and its reflecting pools, symmetry reigns.

It is difficult to think of another tower that combines the height, solidity, and slender elegance of the Qutab Minar (thirteenth century). The reddish stone, contrasting with the transparency of the air and the blue of the sky, gives the monument a vertical dynamism, like a huge rocket aimed at the stars. It is a "victory tower," deeply rooted in the ground, that unbendingly ascends, a prodigious stone tree. It is said that the original construction was the work of Prithiv Raj, the last Hindu ruler of Delhi. The tower was part of a temple that also housed the famous Iron Pillar, which has an inscription from the Gupta period (fourth century).

No less beautiful, but more serene, as if geometry had decided to transform itself into running water and colonnades of trees, is the mausoleum of Emperor Humayum. Like other Muslim mausoleums, nothing about it makes one think of death. The soul of the deceased has disappeared, gone to the other world, and his body has become a small heap of dust. Everything has been transformed into a construction made of cubes, hemispheres, and arcs: the universe reduced to its essential geometric elements. The abolition of time turned into space, space turned into a collection of shapes that are simultaneously solid and light, creations of another space, made of air. Buildings that have lasted for centuries that seem to be a split second of fantasy. What Baudelaire called "the vegetal irregular," a proliferation of the organic, an order that has disappeared, except as a stylization for decorating walls. The mausoleum is like a poem made not of words but of trees, pools, avenues of sand and flowers: strict meters that cross and recross in angles that are obvious but no less surprising rhymes.

In Islamic architecture, nothing is sculptural—exactly the opposite of the Hindu. One of the great attractions of these buildings is that they are surrounded by gardens ruled by a geometry made of variations that regularly repeat themselves. A combination of multicolored expanses and avenues of sand bordered by palms. Between them, huge rectangular pools reflect, according to the hour and the changing light, different aspects of the unmoving buildings and the crossing clouds. Untiring games of light and time, always different and always the same. The water performs a double and magical function: to reflect the world and to scatter it. We see and then we don't see; all that remains is a fistful of fleeting images. There is nothing terrifying in these tombs: they give the sensation of infinity and pacify the soul. The simplicity and harmony of their forms satisfy one of the most profound necessities of the spirit: the longing for order, the love of proportion. At the same time they arouse our fantasies. These monuments and gardens incite us to dream and to fly. They are magic carpets.

I will never forget one afternoon in a tiny mosque I had wandered into by accident. There was no one there. The walls were made of marble and inscribed with passages from the Qur'an. Above, the blue of an impassive and benevolent sky, only interrupted, from time to time, by a flock of green parakeets. I stayed for hours, thinking of nothing. A moment of beatitude, broken finally by the heavy circular flight of the

bats who had appeared with the fading light. Without saying
it, they told me it was time to return to the world. A vision
of the infinite in the blue rectangle of an unbroken sky. Years
later, in Herat, I had a similar experience: not in a mosque
but on the balcony of a ruined minaret. I wanted to preserve
it in a poem. I repeat the last lines here because, perhaps, they
say more simply and clearly what I now want to say as I
remember this experience:

> I did not have the imageless vision,
> I did not see forms whirl until they vanished
> in unmoving clarity,
> the being without substance of the Sufis.
> I did not drink the plenitude of the void [...]
> I saw a blue sky and all the blues,
> from white to green,
> the spread fan of the poplars,
> and on a pine, more air than bird,
> a black and white mynah.
> I saw the world resting on itself.
> I saw the appearances.
> And I named that half hour:
> The Perfection of the Finite.

Despite the brevity of my stay, I made a few friends.
Indians are hospitable and cultivate the forgotten religion
of friendship. Many of these ties still last, though some have
been broken by death. Invited and guided by my friends, I
began to frequent the concerts of music and dance, many
of them in the beautiful gardens of the Delhi of that time.
The two arts half-opened the doors to the legends, myths,
and poetry of India: at the same time they gave me a deeper

understanding of the sculpture that is, in turn, the key to Hindu architecture. It has been said that Gothic architecture is music turned to stone; one could say that Hindu architecture is sculpted dance. But this first time I had only a glimpse of Indian art. My stay was interrupted when it had barely begun. The implacable Minister Tello transferred me to Tokyo. I packed my bags again and took the first available plane. Awaiting me was an experience that was no less fascinating . . . but that is another story.

RETURN

Eleven years later, in 1962, I returned to India as the ambassador from my country. I stayed a little more than six years. It was a happy time: I could read; I wrote several books of poetry and prose; I had a few friends with whom I shared aesthetic, ethical, and intellectual affinities; I could travel through unfamiliar cities in the heart of Asia, witness strange customs, gaze on monuments and landscapes. Most of all, it was there that I met my future wife, Marie José, and there that we were married. It was a second birth. Together we traveled around the subcontinent. On my first trip, I had been able to visit Burma and Thailand. On the second, Vietnam, Cambodia, and Nepal. Moreover, I was simultaneously the ambassador to Ceylon and Afghanistan, so that I spent a great deal of time in both those countries. When the international situation permitted it, we would go by car from New Delhi to Kabul, across Pakistan. We visited Lahore and the other cities various times, and of course the venerable ruins of Taxila. Crossing the Indus River, we would be greeted by groups of poplars, Mediterranean trees waving at us like friends we hadn't seen for a long time. In Peshawar, I had my first encounter with the Pathans, a people of chivalrous warriors. Later, entering Afghanistan, I met nomadic groups like the Khoji and, toward the Soviet border, the Uzbeks. Peshawar was an important city in the history of Buddhism. Many stupas and architectural traces remain in the area, but the religion has disappeared, supplanted by Islam. In the museum we discovered the art of the Kafirs, remarkable sculptors in wood of heroes on foot or on horseback. The Kafirs are an Indo-European people who resisted all invaders for three thousand years, and who appear in one of Kipling's best stories, "The Man Who Would Be King."* We saw similar sculptures in the museum in Kabul, which also once contained remarkable pieces of Greco-Buddhist art. I must use the past tense, for I don't know if the war that has devastated the country has also destroyed these treasures.

From Peshawar to the Khyber Pass: the innumerable invasions over more than three millennia, and yet, in the vague historical remains, the reality of the human imagination: Kipling and his stories, novels, poems. The ancient lands of Gandhara, where armies and religions clashed. What has remained of all that spilled blood, all those religious and philosophical disputes? Barely a handful of fragments: the head of a Bodhisattva that could be an Apollo, a relief broken from a temple, a row of Kushan and Indo-Greek soldiers, some with their faces disfigured by Muslim rage, a torso, a hand, lovely

---

* Today the region that these people inhabit, in the mountains of the Hindu Kush, is called Nuristan (Land of Light). In 1895, it was converted by fire and sword to the religion of the Prophet. *Kafir* means "infidel," and the name that the Muslims gave this region is "Land of the Infidels," Kafiristan. The Kafirs are Indo-Europeans and, until they were conquered by the Afghanis, were polytheists, with a pantheon of gods similar to those of the Greeks, Romans, Celts, and Germans. One curious detail: they used chairs, which were generally unknown in Asian cultures.

pieces of female bodies eroded by the centuries. If one goes deeper into the country, one can see, not far from Bamian, famous for its giant Buddhas, the heap of stones from that which was called the Red City and was completely demolished by Genghis Khan. A visit to Balk (the ancient Bactria) is deceiving: time, wars, and neglect have destroyed even the ruins there. But it is beautiful to cross this country of courtly people, barren mountains, and fertile valleys. Contemplating the Amu-Darya (for Herodotus the Oxus River) and its powerful currents calms the soul: water is more powerful than history. Or as the Chinese poet says: "The empire crumbles, mountains and rivers remain." At that time, the French Archeological Mission had recently discovered the remains of an "Alexandria on the Oxus," another of the cities of that name that Alexander founded in his passage through these lands.

We also traveled a great deal in the south of India: Madras, Mahabalipuram, Madurai, Tanjore, Chidambaram. Many of these names appear in my poems from those years. And the leap, the leaps, to Ceylon, that is now called Sri Lanka. There we visited Kandy, Anuradhapura, and . . . But why go on? Lists are dull, and these, moreover, are meaningless. But for Ceylon I should relate a small anecdote. On one of our visits, Marie José and I stayed in a house that had been lent to us by a friend in Colombo. It was built on a promontory facing the sea; from it one could see the fort of Galle, founded by the Portuguese in the sixteenth century, though the fort itself was built somewhat later by the Dutch. Nearby there is a small cove into which a stream of fresh water flows, blue and white, between the rocks. There the Portuguese ships would stop to replenish their supply. A path leads over a hill to a small village of fishermen and, half hidden in the coconut trees, a tiny

Buddhist temple maintained by a dozen monks, almost all of them young and smiling. The sand on the beach is fine and golden, the water blue, green, translucid; in its depths one can see pink coral formations. A paradisiacal spot and, in those days, deserted. It was a surprise, then, to learn later that Pablo Neruda had lived in this exact spot thirty years before and had, according to a friend, found it abominable.

I have mentioned these names as though they were talismans that, upon being rubbed, bring to life images, faces, landscapes, moments. And they are like certificates: a testimony that my education in India lasted for years and was not confined to books. Although it is far from complete and will remain forever rudimentary, it has marked me deeply. It has been a sentimental, artistic, and spiritual education. Its influence can be seen in my poems, my prose writings, and in my life itself.

During those years, I made various friends. One of them was the novelist and essayist Raja Rao, whom I had met in Paris at the home of the poet Yves Bonnefoy shortly before my second stay in India. That night we discovered that both of us, for different reasons, were interested in the Cathar heresy: he for its philosophical and religious spirit, I for its somewhat tenuous and circumstantial relation with courtly love. We became friends, and on each of his trips to Delhi—he was a professor at an American university—he never failed to visit me. Later we saw each other in different places. The last time was in Austin, Texas, at a festival of poetry. Czeslaw Milosz was also there, another profoundly religious man with a philosophical temperament. Rao and Milosz immediately became friends and launched into long and passionate dialogues. Hearing them, I remembered this fable: After the final battle foretold by the holy books, among the corpses and the rubble, two men appear, the only survivors. One is a Hindu, a follower of Vedānta; the other a Christian, a Thomist. No sooner do they discover each other than they begin to debate. The Christian says: The world is an accident; it was born from the divine *fiat lux;* it was created, and like everything that has a beginning, it will have an end; salvation is beyond time. The Hindu answers: The world had no beginning and will have no end; it is necessary and self-sufficient; change doesn't change it; it is, has been, and will always be identical to itself. And the dialogue continues, the debate never ends. . . .

Late in 1963, I received a telegram from Brussels informing me that I had been awarded the Knokke le Zoute International Prize for Poetry. At that time it was a prestigious award that had been given to Saint-John Perse, Ungaretti, and Jorge Guillén. Not a well-known prize, but among those who knew it—people who truly interested me—it was, more than a distinction, a kind of confirmation. The news disturbed me. Since my adolescence I had written poems and had published various books, but for me poetry had always been a secret religion, celebrated outside the public eye. I had never received a prize for it, and had never wanted one. Prizes were public, poems private. If I accepted the prize, wouldn't I be revealing the secret and betraying myself? I was in this dilemma when I happened to see Raja Rao. I told him my problem. He replied: "I cannot give you advice, but I know someone who can. I'll take you to that person tomorrow, if you like." I accepted, without asking anything further. The next day, early in the afternoon, he came by and took me to a modest house on the outskirts of Delhi. It was an *ashram,* a place for retreat and meditation. The spiritual director was a woman who was well known in certain circles, Mother Ananda Mai.

The ashram was simple, sober rather than severe, and seemed more like a college than a convent. We crossed a small patio with two withered lawns and two small trees. There was an open door, and we entered a small room. There we found about a dozen people sitting on chairs in a semicircle around a woman who was seated on the floor. She was around fifty, dark-skinned, with loose black hair, deep and liquid eyes, thick, well-defined lips, wide nostrils as though made for deep breathing, her body full and powerful, her hands eloquent. She was dressed in a dark-blue cotton sari. Receiving us with a smile—she had known Raja Rao for a long time—she gestured to us to take a seat. The conversation, interrupted by our arrival, continued. She spoke in Hindi, but would answer a foreigner in English. As she spoke, she played with some oranges in a basket next to her. She soon looked at me, smiled, and threw an orange at me, which I caught and held on to. I realized that this was a game, and that the game contained some sort of symbolism. Perhaps she wanted to say that what we call "life" is a game and nothing more. Ananda began to speak in English and said: "I am frequently asked who I am. And I answer you: I am a puppet, the puppet of each one of you. I am what you want me to be. In reality, I am nobody. A woman like any other. But the puppet whom you call Ananda the Mother is your fabrication. I am your toy... Ask me whatever you like, but first I must say that the answer will not be mine, but rather your own. It is like a game in which each person answers himself."

There were various questions—in the group were four or five Europeans and Americans, men and women—and then it was my turn. Before I could speak, Ananda interrupted me: "Raja Rao has already told me about your little problem." "And what do you think?" I said. She began to laugh: "What vanity! Be humble and accept this prize. But accept it knowing that is worth little or nothing, like all prizes. To not accept it is to overvalue it, to give it an importance that it does not have. It would be a presumptuous gesture. A false purity, a mask of pride . . . True disinterest is accepting it with a smile, as you received the orange I threw you. The prize will neither make you nor your poems better. But don't offend those who awarded it to you. You wrote those poems not in the spirit of gain. Do the same now. What matters is not prizes but the way they are received. Disinterest is the only thing that matters. . . ."

An old German woman wanted to ask something more, but Ananda said, "We have ended for today. . . ." I was hoping that, as in other congregations, the session would end with the singing of some hymn. But without ceremony, two assistants invited us to leave. Some people remained on the patio, no doubt hoping for a private interview. Raja Rao took me by the arm and, when we reached our car, asked, "Are you happy?" "Yes, I am," I replied, "not because of the prize, but for what I heard." Rao said, "I don't know if you realized that everything Ananda said is in the *Gītā*." I hadn't known. A few years later, I understood: to give and to receive are identical acts if they are realized with disinterest.

Ananda Mai's words persuaded me to accept the prize. The following year, I was on my way to Belgium to receive it, and I stopped in Paris for a few days. One morning—chance, fate, elective affinities, or whatever one wants to call these encounters—I ran into Marie José. She had left Delhi a few months before, and I didn't know her whereabouts, nor she mine. We saw each other and, a little later, decided to return to India together. I remember that one night, shortly before I left Paris, I told André Breton the story of my unexpected encounter, and he replied by quoting four lines of a mysterious poem by Apollinaire, "The Gypsy":

> We know so well that we are damned,
> But the hope of love along the way,
> Makes us think, hand in hand,
> Of what the Gypsy had to say.

Marie José and I were not enacting the prophecy of a Gypsy, but our meeting was a kind of recognition. To live is to be condemned, but it is also to make choices; a determinism and a freedom. In love's encounter, the two poles entwine into an enigmatic knot; embracing as couples, we embrace our destiny. I was searching for myself, and in that search I found my contradictory complement, that you (*tú*) that becomes I (*yo*), the two syllables of the word "yours" (*tuyo*) . . . But I am not writing a memoir: these pages, although they touch on autobiography, are an introduction to my attempts to answer the question that India poses to everyone who visits it.

My official obligations brought me into contact with various politicians, Nehru among them. It was in the last years of his life. Despite his visible fatigue, I was always amazed at his elegance: immaculately dressed in white with a rose in his lapel. It was not difficult to guess that his two great passions were politics and women. He was an aristocrat, and the years of struggle, prison, debates with colleagues and adversaries, and daily dealings with the masses and with flocks of diplomats hadn't changed his good manners, his bearing, and his smile. In calling him an aristocrat, I am thinking first of his origins —he was a Brahman from Kashmir, son of a well-known and wealthy father, Motilal Nehru—and then of his English education, which became second nature to him. He never learned Hindi, but spoke Urdu and colloquial Hindustani. In 1931, Gandhi had written about him: "He is more English than Indian in his manner of thinking and of dress; he often feels more at ease among the English than among his own countrymen." Nehru was a man of Western culture; neither in his words nor in his thought was there the slightest trace of any sympathy or affinity with the double religious tradition of India, the Hindu and Muslim. He was, however, remarkably interested in young artists: one day, to our surprise, he appeared at an opening in an obscure gallery. It was an exhibition of a group of young iconoclasts headed by the painter J. Swaminathan, for which I had written a short text. In the end came the bitter days: the conflict with China. All of his international policy in those days, as one can see in the speeches of Krishna Menon (whom I think of as Nehru's evil spirit), was directed toward creating an anti-Western front, one wing of which was the organization of nonaligned nations and the other the "socialist" block. Did he ever realize his terrible miscalculation?

I had little contact with Nehru, but I saw his daughter Indira often, first when she became the minister of information at her father's death, and later when she was the prime minister. She would consult me about Latin American political and cultural affairs. A reserved and affable woman, her questions and observations were succinct and, in concrete matters, the opposite of her father. For many years she was his confidante, his right hand, and councilor. A strange mixture of filial piety and political passion that later would become an even more explosive combination: political interests and maternal love. First she promoted and protected her younger son, Sanjay, whom she was carefully preparing as her successor. When Sanjay died in an airplane accident, she transferred her designs to her other son, Rajiv, who succeeded her at her death. Indira belonged to modern democratic culture, but her deepest sentiment was traditional: the family. Although she was not religious, she was possessed by the passion and the belief that she belonged to a predestined lineage— the Brahmans of Kashmir. It was not an idea but a feeling. This passion, in the end, clouded her realism and her sharp political understanding. She had been formed in the internal and external struggles of the Congress Party. This experience and her natural instincts—she had politics in her blood—gave her the ability to overwhelm her adversaries: party veterans and prestigious men like Morarji Desai, who were older than she was and reputed to be master political strategists. But her own cunning ultimately defeated her: to conquer her enemies in the Punjab, who were the members of her own party, she encouraged the extremists who would later assassinate her.

In 1984, sixteen years after leaving India, I was invited to Delhi to give the annual lecture in honor of Jawaharlal Nehru. The invitation had been made at Indira's request. It was a great honor, and moreover gave us the opportunity to return to India. Having been invited also by the Japan Foundation that year, I planned to go first to Japan and then to Delhi. Marie José and I were in Kyoto when we learned that Indira had been assassinated by two of her Sikh bodyguards. The news shocked us. A few days later, with much difficulty, I was able to get through to Delhi. Riots and massacres had followed the crime. It was decided, as might be expected, to suspend the lecture, but the Indian officials insisted that we come for two weeks. We found a country that had been torn apart. For the Sikhs, the Indian government was an accomplice in the Hindu machinations against them. For the Hindus, religious fervor had mixed with nationalism: Sikhism, as a religion, is close to Islam. The brutal scenes of 1947 had been repeated, although for a shorter period of time and limited to Delhi and other Hindu strongholds. The mobs once again took over, killing many Sikhs—the exact number is unknown—and looting their stores. Some of my friends, Punjabis who were not Sikhs, blamed Indira: she had been the first victim of a conflict she herself had provoked. They were right: it seemed clear that Indira, spurred on by the devil of politics, had lit the fire that consumed her. But the deeper truth was and is quite different: one cannot reduce the history of India to any individual. In the past the Indians created a great civilization, but they could never create a unified nation or a national state. The centrifugal forces of India are old and powerful: they have not destroyed the country because, without intending to, they have neutralized one another.

The new Prime Minister, Rajiv Gandhi, renewed the invitation. I gave the lecture in 1985, never imagining that a few years later he too would be assassinated. One night on that visit, our last to India, the writer Sham Lal gathered a group of friends in his house. He had read *Renga*, a poem that had been written in Paris in 1969 by four poets (Charles Tomlinson, Jacques Roubaud, Edoardo Sanguinetti, and myself). It occurred to him that the experiment could be repeated with Hindi poets. We agreed, and sheets of paper were passed out to three of us: Agyeya (S. Vatsyanan), the patriarch of Hindi poetry; Shirkant Verma, a young poet; and myself. Our poem was composed according to the tradition of Hindi and Urdu poetry: a six-line stanza followed by a concluding couplet. The first line was written by me in Spanish; the second and third by Agyeya in Hindi; the fourth and fifth by Verma, also in Hindi; the sixth, again by me, in Spanish. The last two lines, the coda, were written three times, once by each of us, so that the poem would have three different endings. I present it here in memory of Shirkant Verma, who died in his youth:

POEM OF FRIENDSHIP

O. P. Friendship is a river and a ring.

A. The river flows through the ring.
The ring is an island in the river.

S. V. The river says: before there was no river,
after there is only a river.
Before and after: that which erases friendship.

O. P. Erases it? The river flows, forming the ring.

A. Friendship erases time and thus it frees us.
It is a river that, flowing, invents its rings.

S. V. In the sands of the river our tracks are erased.
In the sands we seek the river: where has it
gone?

O. P. We live between oblivion and memory:
this moment
is an island weathered by incessant time.

Eight years later, I stumbled upon the twenty pages of my 1985 lecture, read them again, and realized their inadequacy. I decided first to expand them; later, dissatisfied, I started over from the beginning. The result is this small book. It is not a memoir, but rather an essay that attempts, with a few quick notes, to answer a question that goes beyond personal anecdotes: How does a Mexican writer, at the end of the twentieth century, view the immense reality of India?

These are neither memoirs nor evocations. What I lived and felt during the six years I spent in India is in my book of poems *Ladera este* (*East Slope*).* and in a short prose book, *The Monkey Grammarian*.† A book of poems is a sort of diary in which the author tries to preserve certain exceptional moments, whether joyful or unfortunate. In that sense, this book is nothing more than a long footnote to the poems of *East Slope*. It is their context—not vital, but intellectual.

I realize there are many gaps in this essay. They are not only numerous but immense. For example, I barely speak of Indian literature, particularly of the two great epic poems, the *Mahābhārata* and the *Rāmāyana*. Nor do I mention the stories and fables. The influence of the *Pañchatantra* was enormous in the Arab countries, in Persia, and in Europe. Many of La Fontaine's fables come from Indian sources, and the massive collection *The Ocean of Story* was the prototype for *The Thousand and One Nights*.# In Indian stories, genres that are separate in our tradition combine in surprising ways: the fairy tale and the picaresque novel, didacticism and libertinage. It is a characteristic of the Indian people: frank realism allied

---

* *East Slope* is included in *Collected Poems 1957–1987*, edited by Eliot Weinberger, New Directions, New York, 1987.

† *The Monkey Grammarian*, translated by Helen Lane, Seaver Books, New York, 1981.

Among the selections from *The Ocean of Story* are the "Tales of the Vampire," available in an elegant French translation by Louis Renou (Gallimard, Connaisance de l'Orient, 1963), and a notable translation by Léon Verschaeve called *La cité d'or* published in 1979 in the same series. I should also mention a remarkable collection edited by J. A. B. Van Buitenen called *Tales of Ancient India* (University of Chicago Press, Chicago, 1950).

with delirious fantasy, a refined astuteness with an innocent credulity. Contradictory and constant pairs in the Indian soul, like sensuality and asceticism, the eagerness for material well-being and the cult of poverty and disinterest.

To return to the lacunae in this book: they are numerous, and they range from poetry, philosophy, and history to architecture, sculpture, and painting. The subject, due to its immensity and variety, rebels against synthesis. Moreover, it is beyond my knowledge as well as my intentions. These are merely glimpses of India: signs seen indistinctly, realities perceived between light and shadow. This book is not for the experts. It is the child not of knowledge but of love.

Religions, Castes, Languages

RĀMA AND ALLAH

The first thing that surprised me about India, as it has surprised so many others, was the diversity created by extreme contrast: modernity and antiquity, luxury and poverty, sensuality and asceticism, carelessness and efficiency, gentleness and violence; a multiplicity of castes and languages, gods and rites, customs and ideas, rivers and deserts, plains and mountains, cities and villages, rural and industrial life, centuries apart in time and neighbors in space. But the most remarkable aspect of India, and the one that defines it, is neither political nor economic, but religious: the coexistence of Hinduism and Islam. The presence of the strictest and most extreme form of monotheism alongside the richest and most varied polytheism is, more than a historical paradox, a deep wound. Between Islam and Hinduism there is not only an opposition, but an incompatibility. In one, the theology is rigid and simple; in the other, the variety of doctrines and sects induces a kind of vertigo. A minimum of rites among the Muslims; a proliferation of ceremonies among the Hindus. Hinduism is a conjunction of complicated rituals, while Islam is a clear and simple faith. Islamic monotheism categorically affirms the preeminence of the One: one God, one doctrine, and one brotherhood of believers. Of course, Islam has experienced divisions within itself, but these have been neither as profound nor as numerous as those within Hinduism, which accepts not only a plurality of gods but also of doctrines (*darshanas*), sects, and congregations of believers. Some of these brotherhoods of believers—true religions themselves within the great pluralistic religion of Hinduism—approach Christian monotheism; for example, among the followers of Krishna. Others recall the original polytheism of the Indo-Europeans: worshiping deities who are the guardians of cosmic order, warrior gods, and gods of agriculture and commerce. In one case, a creator god; in the other, the wheel of successive cosmic eras with its procession of gods and civilizations.

The great religious, poetic, legal, and historical books of the Hindus could not be more different from those of the Indian Muslims; nor is there anything similar in their architectural, artistic, and literary styles. Are they two civilizations occupying a single territory, or are they two religions nurtured by a single civilization? It is impossible to say. Hinduism began in India, and it holds an intimate and filial relation with the Vedic religion of the Aryan tribes who settled in the subcontinent in the second millennium before Christ. In contrast, Islam is a religion that came from abroad fully formed, with a theology to which nothing could be added. It came, moreover, as the faith of the foreign armies who, beginning in the eighth century, invaded India. Islam was imposed, but it took root in India and has remained the religion of millions for a thousand years. Despite these centuries of living side by side, the two communities have preserved their separate identities; there has been no fusion of the two. Nevertheless, many things unite them: similar customs, languages, love of the land, cuisine, music, popular art, clothing, and—to cut short a list that could become interminable—history. A history that unites them but also separates them. They have lived together, but their coexistence has been one of rivalry, full of suspicions, threats, and silent resentments that frequently have turned into bloodshed.

The first forays of Muslim soldiers into India were in the year 712, in the province of Sind. These began as looting expeditions but quickly turned into a full-scale invasion. After the occupation of the Punjab, the Sultanate of Delhi was founded in 1206. Until its disappearance in the sixteenth century, it was ruled by various dynasties, all of them of Turkish origin. These conquerors and their descendants left the social fabric almost entirely intact, so that life in the villages and hamlets barely changed. In the cities, however, the ancient ruling groups—Brahmans, Kshatriyas, wealthy merchants— were replaced by a new, Turkish aristocracy. It was a religious, political, and economic upheaval, the consequence of a military victory, but one that did not affect the basic social structures, although many people converted to Islam. The political position of the sultans was a maintenance of the status quo, as the population generally remained Hindu; the conversion by sword, urged by the orthodox, would have led to social chaos. At the same time, the sultans and the nobility "always sought to conserve their position of dominance not only over the natives who were not Muslim, but also over the Indians who had adopted the Islamic faith as well as the Muslim Turks who had come from distant regions."*

The Delhi Sultanate, though wracked by internecine

---

* See S. M. Ikram, *Muslim Civilization in India*, Columbia University Press, New York, 1964.

struggles and the rebellions of ambitious nobles, was the center of the entire Muslim world. Its flourishing coincided with a period of Islamic decadence, and with the catastrophe that ended the Caliphate: the sack of Baghdad by Genghiz Khan's troops in 1258. Many Muslim intellectuals and artists sought refuge in the new capital. Yet, "despite the cultural eminence of [Delhi], it cannot be claimed that the Sultanate is a period marked by that solid scholarship and study of the sciences which distinguished Baghdad and Cordoba."* In essence, Delhi never had an Averroës or an Avicenna. The great creative period of Islam was over. This is one of the historical paradoxes of Muslim India: it flourished at the decline of Islamic civilization. There were, of course, poets of great distinction, such as Amir Khusrau, who wrote in Persian and in Hindi, and important Muslim works of history, a genre practically unknown in Hindu literature. Perhaps even more significant, from the point of view of the relations between the Hindu and Muslim cultures, was music. It is well known that Indian music deeply influenced that of the Arab world and central Asia. Music was one of the things that united the two communities. Exactly the opposite occurred with architecture and painting. Compare Ellora with the Taj Mahal, or the frescoes of Ajanta with Mughal miniatures. These are not distinct artistic styles, but rather two different visions of the world.

As for the conversion of the natives, almost all of the millions who adopted the new faith came from the lower castes. The phenomenon may be explained as the result of three circumstances: first, the new political and military order after the conquest; second, the possibility offered by Islam for one to free oneself from the chain of birth and rebirth (the terrible

---

* S. M. Ikram, *Muslim Civilization in India*.

law of *karma*), a liberation that was not only religious but also social: the converted became part of a fraternity of believers; third, the work of the Muslim missionaries. The Sufis zealously preached in the two areas that today are ruled by officially Islamic states: Pakistan and Bangladesh. In Sufi mysticism there is a pantheistic vein that has certain affinities with Hinduism. During the Delhi Sultanate, between the thirteenth and fourteenth centuries, three Sufi orders emigrated to India.* Its members had a profound influence among the Muslims as well as among the Hindus; many of the former adopted the pantheistic monism of the Hindu poets and mystics: all is God, and to unite with all is to unite with God. A doctrine clearly heretical for orthodox Islam, which has maintained that between God and his creatures there is an uncrossable abyss. The conflict between the orthodoxy (*Sharī'a*) and Sufi mysticism has deeply marked Islamic religious literature. Its case is not unique: there was a similar tension between the Roman Catholic Church and the mystical movements of Western Christianity, from St. Francis of Assisi to St. John of the Cross.

The Sufi tradition, during the Delhi Sultanate, is rich in important figures, such as the famous saint Nīzam ud-din, who is still venerated in a mausoleum in Delhi that also contains the remains of Amir Khusrau, his friend. But although the Sufism of that period did not transgress the limits of orthodoxy, the end of the Sultanate also marked a fusion of Hindu and Sufi mysticism. Among the Hindus, there was a movement of popular devotion to a personal god (*bhakti*). For the believer, this personal deity incarnates the Absolute,

---

* See Peter Hardy, "Islam in Medieval India," in *Sources of Indian Tradition*, 2nd ed., vol. I, edited by Ainslie T. Embree, Columbia University Press, New York, 1988.

and to unite with this god is to reach liberation (*moksha*), or at least to experience the joy of the divine. Not surprisingly, this popular devotion became the source, throughout India, of poems, songs, and dances. But it is poor in philosophical and theological speculation, the opposite of the Brahmanic tradition. In bhakti one reaches the divine not through reason but through love. The three gods whom these sects worshiped were Vishnu, Shiva, and Devi, the great goddess in her various manifestations. The cult of Vishnu, in turn, had two forms: devotion to Krishna or to Rāma, both avatars of the same god.

In these movements in which pantheism blended with the cult of a personal god, it is possible to recognize certain traces of Sufism. The great difference, in my opinion, is that bhakti, although as full of affection and love for God as Sufism, is an impure, a relative, monotheism. Becoming one with Krishna or with the Goddess, the devotee unites with a manifestation of the Absolute, not with a creator God. Krishna is not a unique god, exclusive of others, as Allah is in Islam. Nevertheless, the affirmation that the road to God is neither through ritual, the axis of Hinduism, nor through understanding, the basis of all the darshanas, but through love, has an undeniable similarity to Sufi doctrine.

The philosophical antecedent of Sufism, its origin, is the Spaniard Ibn 'Arabī (1165–1240), who taught the union with God through all His creations. The affinities of Ibn 'Arabī with Neoplatonism are only one aspect of his powerful thought. There is also an exalted eroticism, as expressed in his book of poems, *The Interpreter of Desire*. The union of opposites, whether in logic or in mystical experiences, has both a carnal and a cosmic aspect: the copulation of the feminine and masculine poles of the universe. Both poet and philosopher,

Ibn 'Arabī, it is said, experienced a genuine epiphany in the form of a Persian woman whom he met in Mecca, and who showed him the way toward the union of human and divine love. Love opens the eyes to understanding, and the world of appearances that is this world is transformed into a world of apparitions; everything that we touch and see is divine. This synthesis of pantheism and monotheism, of belief in the divinity of the creation (the world) and belief in a creator God, was the basis, centuries later, of the thought of such great mystic poets of India as Tukaram and Kabīr.

A revealing fact: all these mystic poets wrote and sang in the vernacular languages, not in Sanskrit, Persian or Arabic. Tukaram (1598–1649), who wrote in Marathi, was a Hindu poet who was unafraid to refer to Islam in terms such as these: "The first among the great names is that of Allah...." But he immediately affirms his pantheism: "You are in the One. ... In [the vision of the One] there is no I or you...." The emblematic figure of these movements is a lower-caste poet, a weaver from Benares, Kabīr (1440–1518). Kabīr was of Muslim origin. Unlike the majority of the Hindu poets, he professed a strict deism, no doubt in order to emphasize his attempt at uniting the two religions. He indiscriminately called that unique God by its Islam or Hindu name: Allah or Rāma (Vishnu). Tagore translated Kabīr's poems because he saw in them the failed promise of what India could have become. For a modern historian, Kabīr was "a pioneer of devotional poetry in Hindi, using the vernacular language in order to popularize religious themes taken from both Hindu and Islamic traditions."[*] This is, of course, true, but he was

---

[*] V. Raghavan, "The Way of Devotion," in *Sources of Indian Tradition*, Columbia University Press, New York, 1960.

something more: a great poet. His vision was unitarian: "If God is in the mosque, to whom does this world belong? . . . If Rāma is in the image that you worship, who can know what happens outside? . . . Kabīr is the son of Allah and of Rāma. He is my *guru*, he is my *pīr*." (*Guru* is the Hindu word for a spiritual teacher, *pīr* is the Sufi term.) This powerful movement of popular devotion had no repercussions among the philosophers or the theologians, nor among the politicians of the two religions. It never turned into a new religion or a new politics, though the bhakti movement might have been the nucleus for the union of the two communities and the birth of a new India.

The sixteenth century marked a significant change. In 1526, Bābur, descendent of Tamerlane on his father's side and of Genghiz Khan on his mother's, a great soldier, a skilled organizer, and an interesting writer, founded the Mughal Empire. This was the height of Islamic civilization in India, the sixteenth and seventeenth centuries. Its decadence began at the beginning of the eighteenth. Nevertheless, although weakened and torn apart by internal conflicts, the empire lasted until the nineteenth century, when it was replaced by the British. The tendency toward fragmentation—a permanent aspect of Indian history, and one that the sultans of Delhi continually faced—was especially pronounced during the long decline of the Mughal Empire. The conflicts were not so much religious as the result of the ambitions of individual princes and national rivalries. The relations between Hindus and Muslims never ceased to be tense, but there was a moment of exceptional harmony under the reign of the great emperor Akbar (1556–1605), a figure who is honored by Indians in the way that Ashoka is by Buddhists or Charlemagne by Europeans.

The branch of Islam that still prevails in India is Sunni, which considers itself the orthodoxy and to which the majority of Muslims belong. The Mughals' rise to power was viewed with some alarm by their religious leaders (*ulamās*). It was not easy for the ulamās to forget that the wives of Genghiz Khan had belonged to different faiths, proof of his equanimity toward all religions, nor that Tamerlane had favored the Shī'a heresy. In the case of Akbar, distrust quickly turned into condemnation. His marriage with a Rajput princess* and his appointment of two princes from that same caste as generals in his army scandalized the orthodoxy. Many of Akbar's most loyal officials and functionaries were Hindu, as were some of his closest friends.† The coronation of Prince Salim, who under the name Jahāngīr ascended to the throne at Akbar's death (having been named as heir only shortly before), became possible thanks to the support of the Rajah Man Singh and other Rajput princes. Another of Akbar's acts that defied not only the orthodoxy, but also the practice of all Islamic governments, was the abolition of the tax (*jizya*) that all non-Muslims were required to pay. The politics of tolerance had become a politics of reconciliation.

In his youth, Akbar had been devoted to Persian poetry, especially that of Hāfiz, who was influenced by Sufi pantheism with its exalted eroticism. Perhaps Sufism led Akbar to be interested in other religions. He commissioned translations of

---

* The Rajputs are a warrior caste probably descended from the Hephthalite Huns who invaded India at the end of the fifth century and formed the aristocracy of Rajasthan.

† See Vincent A. Smith, *History of India*, revised by H. G. Rawlinson, Oxford University Press, Oxford and New York, 1951.

the *Atharva Veda*, the *Rāmayana*, and the *Mahābhārata*. In the
city-palace of Fatehpur Sikri—one of the masterpieces of
Islamic architecture—he built the House of Worship (*Ibadat
Khana*) in which theologians and priests of different religions
would gather: Sunni and Shī'a Muslims, Sufis, pandits and
doctors of the scriptures and philosophies of India, followers
of Zoroaster, and Jesuits from Goa. He countered the discon-
tent of many influential Muslims by issuing a decree called
Divine Faith, in which he designated himself as the arbiter of
all religious disputes. But Akbar did not attempt to become
the head of a new religion. His spirit was eclectic and con-
ciliatory, but his intentions were part of a larger design: to
impose the will of the sovereign on all men and all beliefs.

The political dividends of this attitude were enormous and,
in general, beneficial. The Hindus, particularly those of the
higher castes, who previously had been indifferent if not hostile, looked on the Emperor with sympathy and gratitude. At
the same time, he gained the respect and esteem of the theologians, Brahmans, and intellectuals in general. Muslim opinion, however, was largely unfavorable, although it did not
turn into violence. The greatest and most determined enemy
of Akbar's eclecticism was Sheik Ahmad Sirhindī, who was
vehemently opposed to the Sufi pantheism of Ibn 'Arabī and
his followers, and to the idea of a point of convergence for
Hindu and Islamic mysticism. His defense of the orthodoxy
was theological: God, who is ineffable, should not be confused
with His works or with the contemplation of the divine, if
one does not want to end in a kind of nihilism. One must
return to the objective reality of the world and of its creator,
Allah. There is no union with God: Allah remains forever
unreachable, but we can and must love Him, and that love
begins with obedience to His law. There are undeniable sim-

ilarities among the mysticism of Ibn 'Arabī, the negative theology of the Christian mystics, and the void of Nāgārjuna. In
each of these three currents of thought, negation is the way
toward the Absolute.

Sheik Ahmad's arguments had a practical and political dimension. His defense of orthodoxy was also a defense of the
Muslim community and its privileges, especially those enjoyed
by the ulamās and the throne, its functionaries and courtiers.
Obedience to the monarchy is central to Islamic law. (The
same may be said of Islamic historiography, in that it is often
difficult to distinguish between more or less objective accounts and panegyrics to the Sultan or Emperor.) This sub-
servience and the immense prestige Akbar personally held as
a politician, soldier, and enlightened man perhaps explain why
Muslim opposition never escalated into violent rebellion.

The emperor Jahāngīr, Akbar's successor, did not follow
his father's politics of conciliation, but neither did he fall into
its opposite extreme. His reign was a period of tolerance and
coexistence. As in the earlier regimes, the higher-caste
Hindus, whether through military alliances or through their
wealth as merchants or landowners, held posts of distinction.
But there was nothing comparable to the politics of Akbar,
nor was there a popular fusion of the two religions. Jahāngīr
wrote his *Memoirs* in Persian; it has been praised for the live-
liness of its style. He had aesthetic leanings and political skill,
but he was not inspired by grand designs. He loved pleasure
and allowed his empire—like France under Louis XV and
Madame Pompadour—to be governed by his beautiful and
intelligent wife, Nur Jahān. Jahāngīr was succeeded by his son,
Shah Jahān, who, in the tradition of the dynasty, took power
after assassinating his brother and other relatives suspected
of desiring the throne. Shah Jahān is rightly famous for the

architectural works he constructed in Agra, Delhi, and other places. It was a period of artistic splendor, but his last years were full of sorrow and desolation. First, the death of his wife, Mumtāz Mahal, in whose memory he built the famous mausoleum known as the Taj Mahal. His overindulgence in opium weakened his character and his energy, and it united his four sons against him and against each other. Their war of succession erupted while Shah Jahān was still alive. The victor, having killed his three brothers, imprisoned his father in a palace and ascended the throne under the name Aurangzeb.

One of the slain princes, Dārā Shīkoh, deserves mention. He was Shah Jahān's eldest and favorite son, and was destined to succeed him. Neither a politician nor a soldier, he was an intellectual: as a man of action, he failed and lost his life. Educated in the Sufi tradition, he had the same interest in other religions as his grandfather Akbar. The pantheism of Ibn 'Arabī brought him to Hinduism and, although he never abandoned Islam, his works reveal him to be a spirit who was seeking a bridge between the two religions. He was convinced that the link was to be found in the philosophy of the Upanishads, which he called "the most perfect of the divine revelations." His antipathy toward the ulamās and the *mullahs* (the teachers of doctrine and law) was that of a mystic and a free thinker. He praised silence and, in a poem, lampooned the chatter of the clergy:

> In Paradise there are no mullahs,
> one never hears the racket of their discussions and
> debates...

In 1657, Dārā Shīkoh, with the help of a pandit, translated the Upanishads into Persian. A French traveler and Orientalist,

Anquetil du Perron, made a Latin version of Dārā's translation. That version, published in two volumes in 1801 and 1802, was the one that Schopenhauer read. The philosophic influence of that translation has been enormous: on one side, Nietzsche; on the other, Emerson.

Dārā was executed in an ignominious—there is no other word for it—fashion, after having been condemned of heresy. The murder of Dārā and his brothers, cruel as it seems to us, was part of their dynastic tradition. The religious politics of Aurangzeb was, however, a more serious violation: it did not affect merely the individuals of one family, but rather the majority of the people he governed. The execution of Dārā Shīkoh for the crime of heresy was a sign of the fatal direction events would take. The religious question, a strictly spiritual matter since the inauguration of the Sultanate in the eighth century, turned into a matter of life and death.

While never sharing Akbar's eclectic attitude, the Mughal emperors had, from the beginning, accepted the obvious fact that they were ruling immense territories inhabited by idolaters and infidels. Aurangzeb, a Sunni fanatic, proposed the impossible: "to govern a vast empire, composed of a majority of Hindus, conforming to the laws of Islamic asceticism."* Aurangzeb, a man of superior intelligence, unbreakable will, and moral severity, was not above cruelty and duplicity. He was an astute politician and a talented soldier. His tastes were simple, and he frequently condemned the luxury and ostentation of his father, Shah Jahān. The Taj Mahal struck him as a monument to impiety. Nevertheless, his long reign was a series of terrible mistakes, senseless wars, and useless victories. The decline of the empire begins with him.

---

* Vincent A. Smith, *History of India*.

Under Aurangzeb, the breach between Hindus and Muslims became insurmountable. The Emperor restored the hated tax on non-Muslims; he razed temples and built mosques on their foundations; he destroyed the Shī'a princedoms of Golconda and Bilapur; he broke with the Rajputs, the old allies of his ancestors; and he unsuccessfully fought a new Hindu power, the Marathas, led by the fearless and brilliant Shivājī, who was seen by the majority of Hindus as a hero. At Shivājī's death, realizing that the rebellion had not died with its leader, Aurangzeb decided personally to lead his soldiers. He spent the last years of his life fighting in the enemy territory of the Deccan. He died in 1707 at the age of eighty-eight. His reign had lasted half a century, long enough for him to see what his victories, his personal austerity, and his inflexible principles had brought to his empire. Who, one might ask, harmed India more: the libertines Jahāngīr and Shah Jahān or the ascetic Aurangzeb?

The rest is well known: the internecine struggles among the new powers (Sikhs, Marathas), the growing weakness of the empire—now a shadow of itself—and the appearance of a new protagonist, one that did not come from central Asia, like the Turks and Mongols, but from across the sea: the British. Although the new invaders were also monotheists, their hearts were set not on the conversion of the infidels, whether Hindu or Muslim, but on economic and political domination. At first, the activities of the East India Company were essentially commercial, but economics, like religion, is inseparable from politics, and in a short time the Company became a military and political power.

During the period of the decline of the Mughal Empire, from the beginning of the eighteenth century to the middle of the nineteenth, the coexistence of Hindus and Muslims had become less a matter of entrenched opposition as it was under Aurangzeb, but it never reached a state of reconciliation. There were political and military pacts between Hindu and Muslim leaders, all of them provisional and dictated by circumstances; but there were no movements of religious or cultural fusion such as those under Akbar or, at the other extreme, of a Kabīr or a Tukaram. But although Hindus and Muslims continued to be separate and rival entities, the tension between them slackened. I am largely referring to the nobility, the military leaders, and the higher castes in general. The villages and towns had always enjoyed a certain autonomy, both in the observance of their traditional beliefs and in their manner of local self-government (panchayat). Their true enemies were the landowners, the tax collectors, and the bands of soldiers or outlaws—not all that easy to tell apart—who ravaged the countryside. India lived through a century of anarchy and civil wars. Among those attempting to replace the spectral empire of Delhi were Muslim princes, such as those in Oudh in the north and Mysore in the south, Hindus such as the powerful Marathas, and the Sikhs, who were neither Hindu nor Muslim. Above all, there was the East India Company, which excelled in the twin branches of power: diplomacy and war.

The British conquest of India was a colossal historical feat that lasted more than a century and in which a series of extraordinary personalities participated. The first of these was Robert Clive. Clive's successors—particularly Warren Hastings and Lord Wellesley—were models of their kind, simultaneously wise diplomats and remarkable military men. The East India Company increasingly became an instrument of Great Britain's political expansion, and it was decided that it should be directed by a Governor General, appointed by the British government and accountable to a minister of state. The British, however, continued to honor the institution of the Mughal Empire, represented by the elderly Bahādur Shah II, a great lover of Urdu poetry. In May of 1857, a mutiny broke out in the barracks at Meerut, which housed a large number of native troops (Sepoys) under British command. The rebellion quickly spread. The Sepoys, led by Nana Sahib, were joined by many Muslim princes and potentates, the Maratha chiefs, and various rajahs, among them a fearless woman, the Rani of Jhansi. The rebels seized Delhi and named the octogenarian Bahādur Shah as Emperor of Hindustan. The revolt was crushed in less than a year, despite the numerical inferiority of the British troops and their allies. Bahādur died a few years later, in exile in Burma. Much has been written about the causes of the rebellion; none of which were strictly religious, although the Muslims were the predominant participants. (The Mutiny began with rumors that a new type of rifle, distributed among the Sepoys, had been greased with cow fat, an abominable sin for the Hindus, or with pork fat, an impure food for the Muslims.) Its swift collapse is attributable to a lack of unity of purpose and action. Some rebels wanted to reestablish the reign of the Marathas, others the court of Oudh, and so forth.

Once peace was restored, Great Britain formally accepted the responsibility of governing India, which became a viceroyalty. The Governor General was named viceroy. A proclamation by Queen Victoria in November 1858 solemnly guaranteed religious freedom and upheld the right of Indians to serve in the colonial government. This right was the seed for the future independence of India. Religious freedom abolished the link between religion and state, and its most immediate effect was on the Muslims. Viewed with suspicion on account of their active participation in the rebellion, they lost, with one stroke, their traditional privileged position. Various Muslim writers have accused the Viceroyalty of favoring the Hindus and thus intensifying the separation between the two communities. The charge does not strike me as entirely justified. The separation had existed since the founding of the Delhi Sultanate in 1206. With the exception of Akbar, none of the Muslim rulers, for seven centuries, made any real attempt to transform coexistence into a genuine reconciliation. Their religion would not allow it: idolaters must be either converted or exterminated. Nor is tolerance a Hindu virtue, despite what they say about nonviolence: for Hindus, the rest of us—Christians, Muslims, atheists—are all Untouchables, impure creatures.

As for the historical character of the events of 1857, it is revealing that British historians use the word "mutiny," while Indians speak of the "revolt." No less revealing is that none of them uses the word "revolution." It was not one. It is useful to compare the Mutiny (or, more exactly, the mutinies) of 1857 with the Independence of 1947. The first was a rebellion by the old order. It was not a national revolt, because the idea of a nation had not yet penetrated Indian consciousness. Nationhood was a modern concept, imported by the British. The revolt of 1857 was a doomed and chaotic attempt to return things to the way they had been before the British arrived. The Independence of 1947 was the triumph of British ideas and institutions . . . without the British.

I have noted that the religious freedom proclaimed by the British favored the Hindus. First, the privileges for Muslims were abolished, and the Hindu population was exempted from paying a tax simply for not being Muslim. Second, it was much easier for Hindus—especially those of the higher castes, Brahmans and Vaishyas—to live with Christian than Islamic monotheism. The British missionaries did not have the same kind of specific and official relation with the state as did the ulamās and mullahs, and not believing in the Gospels was not an act of rebellion against the government. Moreover, Christian monotheism arrived accompanied by a culture that was, in part, critical of it: science, political philosophy, democracy. This was predicted, however confusedly, by the Bengali novelist and patriot Bankim Chandra Chatterjee, who saw the British victory as a providential act by Vishnu: the annihilation of Muslim power would mean the resurrection of Hinduism. Chaterjee's prophecy was only partially realized: there was not a resurrection of Hinduism, but rather a division of the ancient empire into two nations: India and Pakistan.

I have written perhaps at too great length on the division between Hinduism and Islam. It can't be avoided: the subject is crucial. But I must add that in India there are other religious communities that are not part of either religion. Besides the Christian, Parsi, and Jewish minorities, there are groups whose beliefs lie somewhere between two religions, such as the Sikhs and the Jains. Sikhism is a compromise with Islamic militancy; Jainism, an archaic heresy, is a compromise with Buddhism. Jainism is non-violent, and its relation with Hinduism over the last two thousand years has transformed it into yet another variation of the mother religion. Jainism is not a caste within Hinduism, but neither is it any longer a heterodoxy. The case of the Sikhs, a warrior community, is the opposite. For many years, especially during the massacres of Hindus and Muslims in the period following Independence, the Sikhs were allied with the Indian government. Today an active portion of that community has declared war on the government and on the Hindu majority. The Sikhs are an example of how religious differences senselessly turn into political separatist movements. Finally, there are the tribes and indigenous communities that live at the margins of Hinduism and who are the object of a slow absorption. Hinduism is a conglomeration of beliefs and rituals; although it lacks missionaries, its power of assimilation is immense. It does not know conversion in the Christian or Muslim sense, but it practices, with great success, appropriation. Like an enormous metaphysical boa, Hinduism slowly and relentlessly digests foreign cultures, gods, languages, and beliefs.

THE COSMIC MATRIX

The complexity of India is not limited to the division of Islam and Hinduism and to the profusion of communities, religions, and sects that live among the two great religions. Another element that has always perplexed observers is the institution of castes. It is a phenomenon that is truly unique. Although the caste system bears some similarity to practices in other times and places—for example, in ancient Sparta—nowhere else has it been so complex or lasted so long. It has endured now for at least two thousand years. As far as its complexity is concerned, one need only note that there are more than three thousand castes, each with its own characteristics, gods and rituals, rules of kinship, and taboos of sex and food. No less complicated are the religious and ethical principles that inspired the system, and the ethnic, historic, and economic realities to which it responds.

What are castes, and what was the reason for their creation? I must confess that I find none of the definitions—or the social, economic, and historical causes that have been adduced to explain the phenomenon—entirely satisfying, although in much of the literature I've discovered interesting hypotheses and revealing facts and information. The most original, coherent, and profound explication is that of Louis Dumont.* The paradoxical advantage of Dumont's theory over all the others is that it is not a causal explanation but an anthropological description. He does not tell us why there are castes in India, but rather how they work: their function in a social and ideological system that has given them their characteristics.

For Dumont, castes are, above all, social realities: family, language, trade, profession, territory. At the same time, they are an ideology: a religion, a mythology, an ethic, a kinship system, a set of dietary laws. They are a phenomenon that is explicable only within the Hindu vision of the world and of humanity. It seems to me that Dumont is correct; his theory is impeccable. But I am disturbed by his silence on the origin of the caste system, and without such an explanation every theory is incomplete. With that reservation, I offer a brief synthesis of Dumont's ideas, with a few personal remarks. At the end, I'll return to the subject of the origin of castes.

First, to clarify our thinking, we must be precise about the meaning of the Sanskrit word *varna*. It does not really mean "caste," as was believed for a long time.† It is a term found often in ancient Indian literature, where it may be translated as "color," distinguishing the Aryans from the natives. But it also means "category," "state," "social condition," "position in a hierarchical order." There are four varnas: the Brahmans

---

* Louis Dumont, *Homo Hierarchicus: The Caste System and Its Implications*, University of Chicago Press, Chicago, 1970.

† The Portuguese, faced with the complexity of Hindu social reality in the sixteenth century, were the first to use the word "caste" in the sense of "lineage."

(priests), the Kshatriyas (warriors), the Vaishyas (merchants and businessmen), and the Shūdras (peasants, workers, servants). The two higher categories are composed of individuals who have been born at least twice as humans and thus are superior. The original division, according to Georges Dumézil, was tripartite and corresponded to the three traditional functions of the Indo-European gods: those who rule the cosmic order, those who make war, and those who conserve or maintain the universe through their actions. The fourth varna was added when the Indo-Europeans invaded India in the third millennium B.C. and encountered the indigenous peoples. The four varnas are categories essential to the idea of caste, but they are not its basis.

The Hindu term for caste is *jāti,* which means "species," as in animal or plant species. Or, as the dictionary says, "a group of living beings with common characteristics." The castes themselves are much smaller than the varnas. Various qualities define them. First, origin or blood: one is born into this or that caste. Then, the place or area where one lives; one's trade or profession; kinship rules (a man of caste X may marry a woman of caste Y but not of caste A or Z); diet, which ranges from the strict vegetarianism of the Brahmans to the possibility, among the Untouchables, of eating beef.

Caste must be distinguished from class. For the modern Westerner, the individual is the primary element. A class, a sect, a church, a political party, and even a nation are groups of individuals. This, Tocqueville said, is what distinguishes modern democratic society from the aristocratic societies of the past, where one's birth determined whether one belonged to the nobility, commoners, peasants, or various trades— where the family was the basic unit. In India, the unit, the first and last reality, is the caste.

How is one caste distinguished from another? Unlike our class system, the sign of a caste is religious, not economic or political. Castes, like classes, are elements of a hierarchical totality, but the Western concept of hierarchy is quite different from the one that is the basis of caste. For us, class is associated with power and wealth. The social hierarchies of the West are an order, ranging from superior to inferior, based on domination, whether political or economic. Castes are also part of the Hindu hierarchical system, but the basis of their order is neither power nor money, but rather a religious notion. Like everything that pertains to the realm of the sacred, caste divides into the pure and the impure. There is not a perfect correspondence, as there is in the class system, between caste and one's material situation. The Vaishya, the merchant, may be far richer than the Kshatriya, the warrior. In fact, it has nearly always been that way: there are countless stories of warriors who must get money from the merchants, whether through loans or by force. In turn, it is obvious that the Kshatriya possesses supreme strength, that of the sword; nevertheless, the Brahman is his superior. Of course, membership in a higher caste generally implies a certain degree of economic comfort, higher education, and other material advantages. Yet there are many poor—very poor—Brahmans, and extremely wealthy merchants and businessmen who do not belong to the upper castes. The new middle class of Bombay and Delhi is, for the most part, composed of neither Brahmans nor Kshatriyas. At the same time, many of the Communist leaders in Bengal or Kerala are Brahmans. Nehru was a Brahman, but Gandhi was a Vaishya.

Besides their religious aspect, castes are groups ruled by councils that serve a political function in self-government. Alongside this political autonomy in internal matters, one must add an economic function. Castes are mutual aid societies. They are not only cooperatives, such as ours, but also solidarity groups, genuine fraternities. Each individual is nearly always guaranteed help from other caste members. Furthermore, the ties between members of a caste are also familial. The kinship rules of each caste are extremely complex and strict. Thus, the system is a web not only of economic and political relations but also of families united by marriage: grandparents, aunts and uncles, cousins, nieces and nephews.

This whole complex knot of relations turns around two other axes. The first is trade or profession: there are castes of jewelers, carpenters, weavers, even castes of thieves (the "criminal tribes" of British law). The other axis is territory: each caste is rooted in a certain place, whether a small village or a neighborhood in a metropolis. And place, ultimately, implies language. In sum, this fabric of religious, economic, political, territorial, linguistic, and familial relations gives the castes their extraordinary solidity. Otherwise, their survival for two thousand years would be inexplicable.

The caste, unlike our classes and associations, is not a conglomeration of individuals, but a circle of families. Yet it is a circle that encloses the individual: one is born, lives, and dies within one's caste. There is only one way out of a caste, other than death: renouncing the world. One becomes a hermit or a holy man, walking the roads seminaked and with nothing more than a tin bowl for collecting alms and food. There are perhaps a million of these *sādhus* traveling through India, alone or in small groups, sometimes covered in ashes, and always painted, on their foreheads or chests, with signs—such as Shiva's trident—of the sect to which they belong. One sees many of them in the pilgrimage spots and holy places of Hinduism. Like Christian or Buddhist monks, some are crooks and lunatics, but some are saints. Whatever the case, all have renounced their caste, and with it their families and possessions. In India, as in medieval Europe, there are two types of beggars: the needy—the ill or handicapped—and the religious.

To renounce one's caste is like leaving the maternal belly that warms and shelters us from the outside world. Caste is a protection, but it is not a vehicle for social mobility. This is what distinguishes it radically from all the groups and collectives of modern democratic societies (or semimodern ones, like those in Latin America). Caste does not promote the individual, but the caste itself may change its status. For example, a caste of poor workers may, through some circumstance, increase its wealth and subsequently alter its dietary laws, customs, or even its name. The caste as a whole, rather than any particular individual, can climb the social ladder. (I should add that these cases are exceptional and, like all exceptions, confirm the rule.) Castes were invented not for change, but for endurance. It is a model of social organization for a static society: change destroys its nature. The caste system is ahistorical; its function is to oppose history and its permutations with an immutable reality. Of course, castes change, like everything else in life, but this happens very slowly: one of their central characteristics is their resistance to change.

The opposition between history and caste turns into open hostility when history takes the form of progress and modernity. I am referring not only to democratic liberalism and socialism, but also to their rival, nationalism. Castes constitute a reality that is indifferent to the idea of the nation. Modern Hindu nationalism, as we will see, is a threat to caste because it replaces the specific differences of each caste with an ideological reality that encompasses all. Nationalism erodes the differences among the castes, which are their essential reason for being, as democracy erodes the hierarchical system. Modernity, in its two directions, is incompatible with the caste system. As each individual is to his caste, each caste is to the system: it is a web of interrelations that both unites them and distinguishes one from the other. What unites the castes, and has made them into a true solar system in a slow and perpetual circular motion, is the relations among them. They are relations of Otherness. Each caste is distinct and unique, but all of them revolve around the same immutable principle: the notion of purity that is their origin.

The strength of the system resides in the plurality of its manifestations and in the singularity of the principle that unites them. But the caste system is an obstacle to the modernization of India, that great project that began in the nineteenth century after the contact with British ideas. In 1828, a group of Bengali intellectuals founded a political-religious movement (the Brahmo Samaj, or Divine Society) which was dedicated to purifying Hinduism and, to a certain extent, harmonizing it with modern Christianity. But the caste system is based on the religious and philosophical mainstay of Hinduism: karma. How could one destroy castes without harming Hinduism?

The caste system has resisted two religious attempts at conversion, the Muslim and the Christian. Since Independence, now almost half a century, it has withstood the simultaneous assault of democratic secularism and Hindu nationalism. It has also resisted modern civilization, from the railroads to the factories, where caste distinctions are ignored. Many writers have claimed that the caste system and its static ideology is one of the causes of the poverty of millions of Hindus. It is true, but not entirely true: in other countries in Asia, Africa, and Latin America, where the institution is unknown, misery and terrible inequality also exist. Is there, then, no solution? The answer must be a matter of adaptation. The system is not eternal; nothing human is. Quite probably the castes that the Buddha knew in the sixth century before Christ were not the same as the ones today. I believe that the transformation of the castes and their eventual disappearance will be more rapid in the cities than in the countryside. But the forms this slow process of change will ultimately take are unpredictable.

In the West, since the end of the eighteenth century, change has been overvalued. Traditional India, like the old European societies, prized immutability. For the Indian philosophical tradition, whether Buddhist or Hindu, impermanence is one of the signs of the imperfection of human beings and of all living things. Even the gods themselves are subject to the fatal law of change. One of the values of caste, for traditional Hindu thinking, was precisely its resistance to change. The center of the caste system, I repeat, is religious: the notion of purity. Purity depends, in turn, on the belief in karma: we are responsible for our past lives. Caste is one of the links in the chain of births and rebirths that make up existence, a chain of which all living things are part. Brahmans and Kshatriyas are superior because they have been born as humans at least twice: they have already traveled part of the way on the difficult road of births and deaths.

Preeminence of the collective: the individual is born, lives, and dies in his caste. For us, this condition would be intolerable. Along with change, the modern West glorifies the individual. Without the strength and actions of the individual there can be no change; conversely, without change the individual cannot develop; it would be like a plant denied water or sun. Change and the individual fulfill each other. With his habitual insight, Tocqueville differentiated between egotism and individualism. The first "is born from blind instinct... it is a vice as old as the world and is found in all societies." Individualism, in contrast, was born with democracy, and it tends to separate each person and his family from society. In individualistic societies, the private sphere displaces the public. For the Athenian, the greatest honor was citizenship, which gave him the right to take part in public affairs. The modern citizen defends his privacy, whether it is his religious convictions or economic interests, his philosophy or his property; what counts is himself and his small circle, not the general interests of his city or nation. In aristocratic societies, Tocqueville continues, everyone occupies a fixed position, "one over the other, with the result that each has a superior above, whose protection he needs, and an inferior below, who begs his cooperation. Thus, in the aristocratic societies of the past, people were almost always closely tied to something outside of their own sphere, and were thus more disposed to ignore their own selves."

Tocqueville does not deny the egotism of the aristocracies and their meager interest in the collective good, but he emphasizes their spontaneous sacrifices for other people and for the collective values transmitted by tradition. Aristocratic societies are heroic: the fidelity of the vassal for his lord, the soldier for his faith. These attitudes have almost completely disappeared in the modern world. In democratic societies, where change is continual, the ties that bind the individual with his ancestors have vanished, and those that connect him with his fellow citizens have slackened. Indifference (and, I would add, envy) is one of democracy's great defects. Tocqueville concludes: "Democracy makes each individual not only forget his ancestors, but also neglect his descendants and separate himself from his contemporaries: he is plunged forever into himself and, in the end, is eternally surrounded by the solitude of his own soul." A prophecy that has been utterly fulfilled in our time.

I find modern societies repellent on two accounts. On the one hand, they have taken the human race—a species in which each individual, according to all the philosophies and religions, is a unique being—and turned it into a homogeneous mass: modern humans seem to have all come out of a factory, not a womb. On the other hand, they have made every one of those beings a hermit. Capitalist democracies have created uniformity, not equality, and they have replaced fraternity with a perpetual struggle among individuals. We are scandalized by the cynicism of the Roman emperors who gave the people "bread and circuses," but is that any different from what we are given today by television and the so-called Ministries of Culture? It was once believed that, with the growth of the private sphere, the individual would have more leisure time and would devote it to the arts, reading, and self-reflection. We now know that people don't know what to do with their time. They have become slaves of entertainments that are generally idiotic, and the hours that are not devoted to cash are spent in facile hedonism. I do not condemn the cult of pleasure; I lament the general vulgarity.

I note the evils of contemporary individualism not to defend the caste system but to mitigate a little the hypocritical horror it provokes among our contemporaries. Above all, my goal is not to justify the castes but to give an idea of what they are like. For my part, if I could, I would radically change them. The existence of Untouchables is a disgrace. But castes must not disappear so that its victims may turn into the servants of the voracious gods of individualism, but rather that, between us, we may discover a fraternity.

Dumont does not explain how the institution of castes was born. There are many theories, but to list them would be an enormous task. I would rather offer a handful of impressions and opinions. It is safe to say that the caste system was born as a result of the Aryan migrations into the subcontinent in the second millennium before Christ. Thus the original tripartite division of the varnas: priests, warriors, and merchants (Dumézil). India is an immense cauldron, and whatever falls into it is condemned to remain there forever. For the last two thousand years, those lands have known innumerable migrations and invasions by exceedingly diverse peoples. The plurality of races, languages, and customs, over three millennia, as well as the geographical diversity, changed those tribes and groups into embryos of the division by caste, particularly when confronted with the cohabitation of distinct groups in the same territory. To this one can add the division of labor: there were farmers and carpenters, musicians and blacksmiths, dancers in the temples, and soldiers in the royal palace.

Along with geographical, political, and economic factors— the power or influence of each group, its intellectual or manual skills—one must take into account another factor: religion. Hinduism slowly spread over the entire subcontinent. This took hundreds of years, perhaps as many as two thousand. Brahmanism was combined with native beliefs, but it never lost the distinctive qualities it had inherited from the Vedic religion. Thus present-day Hinduism was formed. I have already noted that Hinduism does not convert individuals; it absorbs communities and tribes, their gods and rites. As Hinduism spread, so did an idea—if it didn't already exist among many of these peoples—that is pivotal to Brahmanism, Buddhism, and other Asian religions: metempsychosis, the transmigration of souls across successive existences, an idea that one also finds in primitive shamanism. Caste was born from the combination of all these ethnic, geographical, historical, and religious factors. It is a social phenomenon whose basis is religious: the idea of purity, which in turn is founded on the karmic law that we are the consequence of our past lives. For that reason, our sufferings are simultaneously real and unreal: we pay our debt and thereby prepare ourselves for a happier reincarnation.

To all this I must add something essential: unlike the Greeks, Romans, or Chinese, ancient India had no notion of history. Time is a dream of Brahma. It is *māyā:* an illusion. Therefore the origin and model of social institutions is not, as among the Greeks and Chinese, in the past. The caste system was not founded by a mythical hero like the Yellow Emperor or by a legendary legislator like Lycurgus. It was born by itself, although by divine, cosmic will, from the soil and subsoil of the society, like a plant. Caste is jāti, and jāti is species. Caste is, in a way, a product of nature. Its model is the natural order with its various animal and plant species. In my book on Claude Lévi-Strauss, I tell how some villagers in the south of India, trying to explain to me the differences between elephants and tigers, described them with caste classifications of kinship and diet: tigers are carnivorous and monogamous, whereas elephants are vegetarians and polygamous. Caste is part of nature and its works, which are themselves reiterations of an immutable law. In the *Bhagavad-Gītā*, the god Krishna tells the hero Arjuna that caste is one of the spokes of the cosmic wheel.

BABEL

The caste system, central to Indian life, is not the only thing that defies the comprehension of the outsider. No less disconcerting is the plurality of languages, some of them Indo-European, others Dravidian, Tibetan, and aboriginal. The Indian Constitution recognizes fourteen languages, but the number is far greater. According to the 1927 *Linguistic Survey of India*,* 179 languages and 544 dialects were spoken at that time. Not only the number but also the complexity of interconnection among language, culture, religion, and ethnic characteristics is overwhelming. The bond between language and religion is particularly close and has, as might be expected, political ramifications. The most striking example is the affinities and oppositions, not infrequently violent, among the speakers of the three languages of the north: Urdu, Hindi, and Hindustani. These relations are set within the great division between Islam and Hinduism. One need only recall that today Urdu is the official language of Pakistan, while Hindi, at least in theory, is that of India.

Urdu was originally the language of the "encampment"— that is, spoken on the outskirts of the palaces of the Muslim princes. It was the language of the public squares and the bazaars. Inside the palaces, they spoke Persian, Arabic, and perhaps other Central Asian languages. Bābur, the first Mughal emperor, was originally from Fargana, a land celebrated in Chinese poetry for its beauty and the agility of its horses. He wrote his famous memoirs in Turkish. Persian,

---

* The most comprehensive and reliable edition on this subject. Censuses taken since Independence are markedly inferior.

however, was the language of the court, and the one in which the Emperor Jahāngīr, Bābur's great-grandson, wrote his own memoirs. It was the official language of the Muslim rulers from the eleventh century, when Lahore was occupied by the troops of the Sultan of Ghazni, until the nineteenth, when Persian was replaced by English. But the true language of the people, including the intellectual and religious elite, was Urdu.

Descended from a vernacular language that comes from Sanskrit, Urdu is a form of western Hindi spoken in the region of Delhi, but with a strong proportion of Persian—and, to a lesser extent, Arabic and Turkish—words. It spread throughout the north of India and what is today Pakistan, and quite quickly became a literary language. The first great poet who wrote in Urdu was Amir Khusrau. The last in this succession of notable poets was Ghalib, the poet of Delhi. Protected by the last Mughal emperor, Ghalib saw and suffered the horrors of the 1857 rebellion. Besides his lyric poetry and an unsuccessful history of the Timurid dynasty—Bābur was a descendent of Tamerlane—Ghalib is the author of vivid and picturesque letters that offer us a glimpse of Delhi in those years, as well as of his own passionate, sarcastic, and sometimes cynical character.*

Hindustani was and is the popular language of the north of India. Like Urdu and Hindi, it derives from Prakrit, one of the languages into which Sanskrit mutated, much as the present-day Romance languages came from Latin. Hindustani syntax is loose, and it contains many English expressions, as well as words from Persian, Arabic, and the various vernac-

---

* Mirza Asadullah Beg Khan Ghalib (1797–1869). See Ralph Russelid and Khursidul Islam, *Ghalib: Life and Letters*, Harvard University Press, Cambridge, MA, 1969.

ulars of the subcontinent: a true lingua franca. As for Hindi, it is composed of a variety of languages and dialects that have slowly come together. Decisive in this process of unification were, first, the Hindu religious communities, and later, after Independence, official government acts and the support of many Indian intellectuals. Unlike Urdu and Hindi, Hindustani does not have a written literature, but it has been the spoken language of the majority of Indians in the north of the country. For that reason, when the Congress Party was first discussing the question of what the national language should be, Gandhi was inclined toward Hindustani. Nehru also favored this solution, but, loyal to his ideas of the modernization of India, he always insisted that English have the dominant role as the language of administration, and be the instrument of culture, science, and philosophy. Keeping English alive, he thought, would leave the door open to the West.

Hindustani was defeated in the Congress under pressure from the ultra-nationalist groups, among them that of the celebrated and influential Subhas Chandra Bose, who soon after would die fighting the English as an ally of the Japanese. The decision to make Hindi the national language threw oil on the fire of the conflict with the Muslims. For them, the traditional and national language had been Urdu, which moreover was spoken by more people than Hindi. Nevertheless, a few years later, the Constitutional Assembly approved the motion to make Hindi the national language. An unwise decision, and one that is impossible to defend: Hindi is a foreign language in the south of India, in the Deccan, in Bengal—in short, in most of the country. Fortunately, various factors have prevented the fulfillment of this constitutional mandate. But the immediate effect was the displacement of Urdu. In some circles, to speak in Urdu was almost a heresy, yet it was the only Indian language that Nehru knew properly. It remains the dominant language of certain regions and is spoken by tens of millions.

An exactly inverse solution was adopted in Pakistan. There, Urdu is the national language and to speak in Hindi is a double offense: against the nation and against the faith. In both countries, the solution was tainted with political nationalism and religious intolerance. The Hindi that has been imposed on present-day India has yet a further disadvantage: it is a language that has suppressed foreign voices, whether English, Persian or Arabic; in their place it has inserted Sanskrit neologisms. It is as though the English were to purge their language of all words of French origin because they are relics of the Norman invasion. The truth is that very few people fully understand official Hindi, which has become an affected and bureaucratic dialect. In order for "High Hindi" (as some call it, sarcastically) to become a living language, it must submerge itself in popular speech and accept the voices of outsiders, no matter what their origin. Living languages are hybrids and impure.

The linguistic map shows that the triumph of Hindi has been relative. Apart from Western and Eastern Hindi, there are other Indo-European languages of great importance in northern and central India, such as Punjabi, Rajasthani, Bihari, Oriya, Marathi, and, finally, Bengali—a cultured language with a great literary history. In the south, the Dravidian languages, also rich in literature, predominate: Tamil, Telugu, Kanada, Mayalayam, and others. In the northeast and northwest, there are various languages in the Tibetan family (such as those in Ladakh and Assam), not to mention the ancient aboriginal languages.

The linguistic problem of India is, in itself, a political and cultural problem: How can so many millions of people, speaking so many and such different languages possibly understand one another? How can this immense population be educated without a common cultural language? Under the Mughal Empire, the official language was Persian. But Persian was never a popular language: in the north the lingua franca was Hindustani. In the rest of the country they spoke (and still speak) other vernacular languages. The British Empire, for the first time in Indian history, united all the people under its domain, something their predecessors—the Mauryas, the Guptas, the Mughals—could never achieve. This was the great historical accomplishment of the British: to bring a single government and a single law to all the Indian nations. English became not only the official language but also the means of communication among the speakers of all the various languages. With Independence, the linguistic question revealed its terrible contradictory truth: What is or could be the national language of India? The Congress decided it would be Hindi, a language that was never spoken, and never will be spoken, by a majority of the people. As a solution that was intended to be temporary but has lasted for half a century, the true language for government and mutual comprehension among all these peoples has been English. An English that, by the laws of natural history, has increasingly turned into Anglo-Indian. I will return to the subject later. For the moment, I end this chapter with a question: How is it possible to turn this conglomeration of peoples, religions, castes, and languages into a true nation? I will attempt to answer the question in the following chapter.

A Project of Nationhood

FEASTS AND FASTS

India is an ethnographic and historical museum. But it is a living museum, one in which the most modern modernity coexists with archaicisms that have survived for millennia. As such, India is a reality that is far easier to delineate than to define. Faced with such diversity, we can legitimately ask if India is indeed a nation. The answer is not simple. On the one hand, India is a conglomeration of peoples, cultures, languages, and religions; on the other, it is a territory under the dominion of a state regulated by a national constitution. In this sense, one might say that India, as Jayaprakash Narayan once said, is "a nation in the making."

A nation is, first of all, a land and a society united by a legacy—language, culture, religion—and also by a national project. India is not one civilization, but two: Hindu and Islamic. Both are collections of traditional societies in which religion is the center of daily communal life. A religion that is mixed with the practices, languages, and patriotism of each group. These societies, both Hindu and Muslim, have experienced and continue to experience numerous changes caused by various influences, among them technology and modern economics, yet they remain faithful to their traditions. At the same time, alongside these traditional societies is a modern state that proclaims itself as national and is obeyed throughout the country, despite the many, and sometimes violent, separatist movements. This is an enormous historical contradiction. To understand it is to begin to understand, if only a little, the reality of India.

The Indian state is not an isolated entity. Besides existing through the tacit consent of the majority of the people, it is the expression of the will of various groups that, despite their differences, have agreed to the central idea of what I have called the "national project": to create a true nation out of a conglomeration of peoples. This project was born in the nineteenth century among the intellectual elite, chiefly in Bengal, and was the result of philosophical and political ideas imported by the British. Imperialism brought its own negation: the Gospels and democracy, intellectual criticism and nationalism. Besides this intellectual and political elite, who have been the historical protagonists of India for over a century, one must also note the emergence of a new middle class in the principal cities. This class—without much culture and with no great sense of tradition—is, as in the rest of the world, enamored of technology and the values of individualism, especially in its American version. This class is destined to have more and more influence on the society. A strange situation: the middle class, in India and on the rest of the planet, disdains public life and cultivates the private sphere—business, family, personal pleasures—and yet they increasingly determine the course of history. They are the children of television.

The traditional elites, heirs of the awakenings of the first half of the century, are composed of intellectuals and politicians. In politics, they are now largely represented by the generation of Rajiv Gandhi and his successors, whether in the government or in the opposition. Among them, unlike their fathers and grandfathers, ideology has little weight. One exception—and an exception of great importance: Hindu nationalism, in which ideology is the determining factor. The same may be said about the other dissident minorities in the Punjab (Sikhs), Assam, and in Tamil Nadu. The pragmatism of the current leaders of the Congress Party is in itself positive, but pragmatism, by being more realistic than it is—if indeed it is realistic—ought not to abandon the double legacy left by the founders of the Republic: secularism and democracy. Without that legacy, the aggressive Hindu (or, more exactly, Hinduist) nationalism could take control and destroy the Indian nation. Among the intellectuals are many of great distinction: the Indian elite, since the beginning of the last century, has assimilated Western science and culture, in its English version, with intelligence and originality. It has continued to produce mathematicians, physicists, biologists, and historians of the first order, not to mention great poets such as Tagore. Many Indian writers work in English and are rightly esteemed for their novels and stories. I am thinking, of course, of Salman Rushdie, but also of less celebrated writers, such as R. K. Narayan, N. C. Chaudhuri, and Ved Mehta. The preeminence of Indian literature written in English is due not only to the literary merits of the work, which these writers have in abundance, but also to its accessibility.

To continue: Besides being a civilization, India is a state, heir to the British Raj; next, it is an enormous democracy. In reality, from a historical and political perspective, India is a Commonwealth, a confederation or union of peoples and nations; one that is always in danger of fragmentation, but which, since the tragedy of the 1947 Partition, has resisted its centrifugal tendencies. In this sense, the Constitution of India was founded on a fiction: it is not a reality but a blueprint. Yet this fiction has withstood the successive separatist movements that have threatened it. It is a fiction that possesses a historical and political reality of unexpected vitality, a project created by a minority that has shown itself capable of successfully confronting an ancient tradition of internecine wars. This fact merits reflection.

The idea of nationhood—not the reality—is relatively modern. It is often said that the United States is the first modern nation, and the one with which modernity begins. This is, of course, true, but it is frequently forgotten that the United States represents the first time that a people consciously and deliberately proposed itself to be a nation. The French revolutionaries, who used and abused the word "nation," followed the Americans in this. The French movement was a true revolution: the change from one regime to another. But the historical reality called France existed before the Revolution and continued after it. In the United States, before its independence, there was not, strictly speaking, a nation. The so-called American Revolution was a birth: a new nation sprouting from the will of the people. Whereas the English, French, Germans, Italians, and other Europeans are the children of their respective traditions, the Americans invented their own tradition. The cornerstone of the United States is not the past but—a great historical paradox—the future. Its Constitution does not recognize an earlier reality; it is an authentic act of foundation and creation. The example of the United States was recognized by many other peoples: among them, those of Latin America. Although the idea of founding a nation came to India via England, its origin was in the United States. Compared to the American model, the Indian project of nationhood must deal with far greater difficulties. First, the existence of an ancient past, rich in traditions and creations. Then, the heterogeneity of that past: religions, languages, diverse and sometimes warring traditions. I will consider first the second difference, the more obvious one, and then the first.

The Anglo-Americans resolved the problem of heterogeneity with the "melting pot": the fusion of all the races, languages, and cultures into one, under the authority of the same laws and the same language, English. The experiment worked in the nineteenth century and the first half of the twentieth, but today it is in crisis, as we all know. But it is a crisis that does not affect the basis of the experiment: all the ethnic minorities (except for a handful of Mexicans) speak English; all enjoy certain constitutional rights, and all are believers in the "American way of life" (though no one knows exactly what that means). The minorities do not have separatist movements; on the contrary, they are attempting to achieve, within the nation, conditions equal to those of the minorities of European origin. The Indians, on their part, resolved this question though the caste system, which has allowed the coexistence of many peoples and communities under a single hierarchy, though it is clear that caste is a great obstacle to modernity.

The other great difference between the United States and India is in their attitudes toward the past. I have already said that the United States was not founded on a common tradition, as has been the case elsewhere, but on the notion of creating a common future. For modern India, as it is for Mexico, the national project, the future to be realized, implies a critique of the past. In the United States, the past of each of its ethnic groups is a private matter; the country itself has no past. It was born with modernity; it is modernity. In contrast, modernization has been the core of the national project of the Indian elites. The similarity here to Mexico is notable: in both cases we are confronting a project hostile to our own traditions. Modernization begins by being a critique of our past.

In Mexico, that critique was undertaken by the liberals of the nineteenth century, who were influenced by French thinking and the example of the United States; in India, it was the work of their first modern intellectuals, primarily Bengalis, who assimilated English culture in the nineteenth century. The critique in both countries was and is ambiguous: it is a break with the past and an attempt to salvage it. In both Mexico and India there have been intelligent and eloquent defenders of the non-European cultural traditions. This is natural: both countries have rich pasts which are alive today, particularly in India. In Mexico, the pre-Hispanic civilization was destroyed, and what survives are its remnants; in India, the ancient civilization is a reality that encompasses and permeates all aspects of life. The influence of the past has been decisive in the modern history of India. Gandhi saw this clearly. Both a politician and a religious man, he wanted to change India, but not in the way of the modern West; his was an idealized version of Hindu civilization. In short, India's project of nationhood confronts realities that seem invincible, and it contains a deep contradiction: it views the past as an obstacle even as it exalts and hopes to salvage it.

For two hundred years, we Mexicans have debated this same dilemma, although our problems cannot be compared in magnitude or complexity with those of India. Conquest and conversion united the various pre-Hispanic peoples; today the great majority of Mexicans are Catholic and speak Spanish, and even the small islands of pre-Hispanic cultures have been Christianized. The question that faces Mexico is how to make the leap to modernity without having gone through the cultural and political experiences of the eighteenth and nineteenth centuries that radically changed the Europeans and Americans and that form the basis of modernity. In India the question is different, first because of the antiquity and heterogeneity of that past, and second due to its vastness: hundreds of millions of individuals with different languages and traditions. The diversity, however, masks a profound unity: that of a civilization into which another, foreign civilization was inserted, and with which it has lived for over a thousand years without blending into it.

I have mentioned certain similarities and differences between India and Mexico. Here I would like to break the thread of my argument with a digression on some of the specific characteristics that unite and separate the two countries. I beg the indulgence of the reader for this digression, but I am, after all, a Mexican. . . . During the years I lived in India, I noticed that Indians are very conscious of their difference from other people. It is an attitude shared by Mexicans. A consciousness that includes, for Indians, their difference from the other Southeast Asian nations, and, for us, from the other Latin Americans. It would not be an exaggeration to say that the fact of being Mexican helped me to see the difference of being Indian—from the difference of being Mexican. They are not the same, of course, but they are a single point of view. To a certain extent, I can understand what it means to be Indian because I am Mexican.

Apart from this consciousness of our difference, everything else separates us. There are, however, a few surprising similarities in our practices and customs. For example, the prominence of chilies in both Indian and Mexican cooking. In the global gastronomic geography the two cuisines share a single place that can only be called eccentric: they are both imaginative and passionate infractions of the two great canons of taste, French and Chinese cuisine. The word *chili* is of Nahuatl origin; the plant originally came from the Americas. Thus it is a Mexican export. My friend Sham Lal, who studied the ancient cuisine of India, told me that in the classical literary texts there is not a single mention of chilies. When did chili—or more exactly, the many kinds of chilies—arrive in India and become the essential component of its curries? Did it arrive through the Philippines, Cochin, or Goa? Another food probably of Mexican origin is the fruit known in India by its Spanish name: *chico*. In Mexico, its full name is *chicozapote*. In Cochin and in other parts of the south, Indians call it by a variation of its Mexican name: *zapota*. Conversely, the mango is a fruit and a word (it comes from Tamil) that originated in India. In Mexico, the most highly esteemed mangoes are still called "mangoes of Manila." As for curry: in Travancore and elsewhere in the south of India, they designate a certain class of curries with the name *mola,* which seems to be a corruption of our *mole,* as *zapota* is of *zapote. Mole* comes from *muli,* "sauce" in Nahuatl. There is an undeniable similarity between curry and mole: the combination of the sweet and the spicy, the reddish color full of sumptuous reflections, and its accompaniment to a meat or vegetable. Mole was invented in a convent in Puebla in the seventeenth century. Is it an ingenious Mexican version of curry, or is curry a Hindu adaptation of a Mexican sauce? Our perplexity increases when we consider that there is not one but many kinds of curries and moles. Another culinary similarity: instead of bread, Indians eat a kind of tortillas, called "chapatis," that are very similar to ours, though made from wheat flour instead of corn. The chapati, like the tortilla, serves as a spoon: an edible spoon!

If we move from food to clothing, one immediately thinks of the *China Poblana*, the "Chinese" woman from Puebla whose lavish dress became a Mexican national symbol. In New Spain, all Asians were called "Chinese," whether they came from China, Japan, the Philippines, or India. During this period there was a great deal of trade across the Pacific. It has been said that the costume of the China Poblana is an adaptation of the clothes worn by Gujarati women, which reached Mexico through Cochin and the Philippines. The theory is not improbable, but needs further proof. Mole and the China Poblana, both from Puebla, evoke, in turn, the enigmatic figure of Catarina de San Juan, about whom the Mexican historian Francisco de la Maza has written a curious book. Its title tells the story: *Catarina de San Juan: Princess of India and Visionary of Puebla*. Catarina de San Juan was a religious woman of the seventeenth century, famous for her visions, which she related to her Jesuit confessors and spiritual guides. She was venerated by many devotees, clergy and non-clergy alike, who were moved by her austerities and conversations with celestial beings. She was almost beatified, but the Church halted the process and even prohibited her cult. She is buried in Puebla, in the chapel of the Convent of Santa Clara—the same convent, by a strange coincidence, where, in the same century, mole was invented.

Catarina de San Juan came from India. According to her Jesuit biographers, she was a native of Delhi. But the descriptions she gave of her city are so fantastic that it is impossible to know whether she was talking about Delhi or somewhere else. The same may be said of her family origins: she claimed to be a descendant of the Great Mughal. (At that time, Aurangzeb, a fervent Muslim, occupied the throne of Delhi.) Catarina said that her mother's name was Borta and her own, before baptism, was Mirra. Borta does not seem to be an Indian name; Mirra is Greco-Latin, but may be a corruption of Mira, the diminutive of the Indian name Mirabai. The contemporary accounts we have of Catarina de San Juan are doubly unreliable, thanks to the indiscriminate ardor of her panegyrists, as well as to the fact that she herself couldn't speak Spanish very well, nor could she read or write it. What is undeniable is that Catarina was kidnapped, at the age of eight or ten, by pirates on the west coast of India. She lived for a while in Cochin as a slave. Then she was taken to Manila, and sold and shipped to Acapulco. She arrived in Puebla in 1621. She had been bought by a wealthy, devout, and childless couple with whom she lived until they both died. Although officially their slave, she served as their companion and spiritual guide. This is not the place to relate all of her curious story: her unconsummated, "paper" marriage with a Chinese man (a common custom in India), her religious visions, her fame, and, after her death, the attempts by the Church to erase her memory. The words and deeds of Catarina do not reveal any knowledge of Hinduism or Islam; they belong to the faith of the seventeenth-century Baroque. But we lack a modern and more complete study of her: De la Maza is an excellent guide to Mexican colonial history, but he knows little about Indian culture.

In the stories of her visions, Catarina frequently mentions the visits made by Our Lord Jesus Christ to her poor cell. (She spent her last years in a convent but was never ordained as a nun.) She describes these as though they were the visits of a lover; clearly she saw her relationship with Jesus as an amorous one. Such confusion of sentiments is not unusual in Catholicism, particularly in the sixteenth and seventeenth centuries. The greatest example of this tendency is the poetry of St. John of the Cross. But it is impossible not to recall that a similar tradition—and one even more powerful and sexually explicit—has existed in India, among the devotees of Krishna as well as among the Sufis. Although the experiences of Catarina are pedestrian—her confessions are like the dialogues of a young lady with her beaus—they inevitably recall the love of Krishna with a lower-class mortal, the cowgirl Rādhā. Catarina's descriptions are not sensual, but rather sentimental and sugared. Among the visions she told her confessors was one where the Virgin Mary appeared and reprimanded her with a frown for her intimacies with the Lord. Then Jesus appeared to soothe her, telling her not to worry about the Virgin's jealousy. This seems to me neither Catholic nor Muslim, but it is Hindu: a goddess suffering from jealousy. In any case, it is significant—or more precisely, emblematic—that Catarina de San Juan, the most important religious visionary of Mexico's colonial period, was born a Hindu.

Food, more than mystical speculations, is a reliable way to approach a people and its culture. I have mentioned that many of the flavors of Indian food are the same as Mexican. There is, however, one essential difference, not in flavor but in presentation: Mexican cuisine consists of a succession of dishes. This is probably due to Spanish influence. In European cooking, the order of the dishes is quite precise. It is a diachronic cuisine, as Claude Lévi-Strauss has said, in which the dishes follow one after the other in a sort of parade interrupted by brief pauses. It is a succession that evokes the image of a military march or a religious procession. It is in itself a *theory,* in the philosophical meaning of the word: European cuisine is a *demonstration.* Mexican cooking obeys the same logic, but not with the same rigor: it is a mixed cuisine. In it, another aesthetic intervenes: the contrast, for example, between the spicy and the sweet. It is an order violated or punctuated by a certain exoticism. A radical difference: in India, the various dishes come together on a single large plate. Neither a succession nor a parade, but a conglomeration and superimposition of things and tastes: a synchronic cuisine. A fusion of flavors, a fusion of times.

If we pause for a moment over the history of India, we find that this too distinguishes it from other civilizations: more than a succession of epochs, its history has been a superimposition of peoples, religions, institutions, and languages. If we move from history to culture, the same phenomenon appears: not only a plurality of doctrines, gods, rites, cosmologies, and sects, but also conglomeration and juxtaposition. In Vishnuism it is not difficult to find echoes and reminders of Shivaites, Buddhists, and Jains; in the movement of intense devotion to a god (bhakti), there are clearly discernible traces of Sufism. In the Shivaism of Kashmir there are Sufi resonances; for example in Lallā, a woman prophet of the fourteenth century. In the poems she has left us, yoga unites with the exalted erotic mysticism of the Sufi poets:

Dance, Lallā, dressed only in air;
sing, Lallā, covered only by sky.
Air and sky: is there any robe more beautiful?

In Indian cuisine, one is astonished equally by the diversity of flavors and their conglomeration on a single plate and by the number and rigor of its ritual taboos, from the prohibition of using one's left hand to the rule of eating only milk and dairy products. At one extreme, the banquet; at the other, the fast. The Indian dietary regimen is a panoply of prohibitions: for certain castes, usually the highest Brahmans, the taboo against meat extends to fish and eggs; for others, it only includes beef. Against the succulence of certain dishes and the variety of sauces, the frequent fasts and the severity of diets. I knew a prominent leader of the Congress Party, a colleague of Gandhi and Nehru and an able minister of finance, who subsisted solely on nuts, yogurt, and fruit juice. Much like fasting, certain meals themselves have religious connotations. I am thinking particularly of the Tantric feast, a ritual meal among certain sects where foods are mixed in forbidden combinations, beef is eaten, alcohol is drunk, or hallucinogenic drugs are taken. The ceremony ends with ritual copulation among the participants, men and women. These ceremonies take place at night, sometimes in the places where the dead are cremated.

Equivalent to the dietary restrictions are the rules that govern each caste in its relations with other castes. In both, separation is rigorous. A duality: the Tantric feast is the central part of a sexual rite and thus the exact counterpart of the fasts and chastity practiced by other devotees. They are the two extremes of Hindu religious life, like two mirrors facing each other with opposite images. In the realm of culture, the equivalent of the dietary, social, and religious prohibitions is the love of classifications and distinctions, grammatical as well as conceptual. One of the glories of Hindu civilization is Pānini's treatises on grammar; less remembered but no less important for both Hindus and Buddhists is his work on logic. Alongside this scrupulous love for distinctions and categories, however, are the confused tales of the Purānas.

One might say that Hindu civilization is the theater of a

dialogue between One and Zero, being and emptiness, Yes and No. Within each system, from thinking to cooking, arises its negation, its criticism. In its most extreme forms, this negation implies a total rupture. The *sannyāsi* abandons his caste, his family, his property, and his city to become a wandering ascetic. The fast negates the feast, the silence of the mystic negates the words of the poet and the philosopher. Zero, the negation, in Buddhism takes the form of the Void. In philosophy, which was as closely associated with religion as our medieval scholasticism, the differences among the six traditional schools (*darshanas*) is epitomized by the debate between the Sāmkhya school and Vedānta. For the former, the world is divided into a plurality of individual souls and a single, unique substance, the beginning and end of all that exists, an immense matrix of the universe. For the Vedantists, subject and object, the individual soul and the soul of the universe, are two aspects of the same reality: a triumph of the most rigorous monism. In its first stage, Buddhism postulated a radical pluralism, quite close to Sāmkhya: there is no subject, only transitory and evanescent states. In its second stage, that of Nāgārjuna and other philosophers, Buddhist pluralism turned into a sort of paradoxical monism, under the sign opposite to that of Vedānta: not Being, but Emptiness.

Hindu religion is the result of a few thousand years of evolution. Its canonical and doctrinal origin is the religion of the Aryan groups whose beliefs were codified in the sacred texts: the four Vedas, the Brāhmanas, and the Upanishads. In the course of the centuries, this religion experienced great changes. Among the most influential was yoga, a movement probably of pre-Aryan origin. At the same time, Hinduism suffered two excisions: Buddhism and Jainism. The former became a universal religion; the latter is still alive, but is strictly associated with Hinduism. Throughout the centuries, the Brahmanic religion produced complex philosophic systems and, above all, two great epic poems, the *Mahābhārata* and the *Rāmāyana*. The former is a moving epic history of the struggles that divide a family of princes, a verbal cosmos that contains one of the most beautiful and profound texts of world literature: the *Bhagavad-Gītā* (The Song to the Lord).

The duration of Hinduism, as well as that of the civilization that created it, would have been impossible without the criticism and exegesis of the six major philosophical tendencies, and without Buddhism's great negation. This internal criticism fortified and revitalized Indian religion, which otherwise would have degenerated into an unformed mass of beliefs, rites, and myths. Against the threat of conglomeration, which ends in chaos or petrification, India raised a barrier of criticism, exegesis, logical distinctions, and negation. But Hindu thought came to a halt, the victim of a kind of paralysis, toward the end of the thirteenth century, the period when the last of the great temples were erected. This historical paralysis coincides with two other important phenomena: the extinction of Buddhism and the victory of Islam in Delhi and other places. The claim that Buddhism was eradicated by Islamic violence—the Muslim soldiers razing the monasteries and slaughtering the monks—is only partially true. For centuries before, Chinese pilgrims had observed a general moral and intellectual decline among the Indian Buddhists. What is most likely is that the majority of believers, after the disappearance of the monasteries, adopted Hinduism. It was a return to the mother religion.

Faced with Islam, Hinduism withdrew into itself. It lacked the necessary components to wage a religious battle: a church and a state. Moreover, it had withered spiritually, turning into a series of rites and superstitions. At the end of internal criticism and the negations that had made Brahmanism a creative religion, the great lethargy of Hindu civilization began, a lethargy that persists today. Islam, for its part, arrived on the subcontinent as a religion that was already complete, with a theology and a mysticism. India owes to Islam some sublime works of art, particularly in architecture and, to a lesser degree, in painting, but not a single new or original thought. It would take centuries, and the appearance of another great monotheism, Christianity, before Hindus and Muslims would begin to awake.

THE SINGULARITY OF INDIAN HISTORY

This long gastronomical and philosophical divagation has brought me to the point where I began. But in order to understand a little more clearly the nature of the contradiction between the project of the nation that is India and its history, it might be worthwhile to note the singularities of the latter. Yet another detour is inevitable. A recurrent theme of Indian history is the clash of civilizations. Here it seems to me not irrelevant to compare those conflicts with the ones that Mexico has suffered. One last comment, before beginning these reflections: I have always marveled at the world's diversity of cultures and civilizations; nevertheless, much as I find barbarous the belief that one race is superior to another, treating all cultures as the same strikes me as a modern superstition. I deeply admire the originality of the Mesoamerican and Incan civilizations, but I recognize the fact that neither of the two has given us creations comparable to the Upanishads, the *Bhagavad-Gītā,* or the Sermon at Sarnath. My comparisons, whether with the West or with Mexico, are not evaluations.

The antiquity of Indian civilization is enormous: while the Indus Valley civilization flourished between 2500 and 1700 B.C., the "mother" culture of Mesoamerica, the Olmecs, developed between 1000 B.C. and 300 A.D. Another, even more important difference: the Mesoamerican cultures were born and grew in total isolation until the sixteenth century. India, in contrast, was always in communication with other peoples and cultures of the Old World: first with Mesopotamia, and later with the Persians, Greeks, Kuchans, Romans, Chinese, Afghans, Mongols. The thought, religions, and art of India were adopted by many Asian peoples; in turn, the Indians absorbed and transformed the ideas and creations of other cultures. The Mexican peoples did not experience anything like the penetration of Buddhism into Ceylon, China, Korea, Japan, and Southeast Asia, or the influence of Greek and Roman sculpture on Indian art, or the mutual borrowings among Christianity, Buddhism, and Zoroastrianism. The Mexican cultures lived in an immense historical solitude; they never knew the essential and common experience of the Old World: the presence of the Other, the intrusion of strange civilizations with their gods, technical skills, visions of this world and the next.

Compared to the diversity of the Old World, the homogeneity of the Mexican cultures is astonishing. The image that Mesoamerican history presents, from its origins until the arrival of the Spanish in the sixteenth century, is that of a circle. Time and again these peoples, for two millennia, began and began again, with the same ideas, beliefs, and technologies, the same history. Not an immobility, but rather a revolving in which each epoch was simultaneously an ending and a new beginning. Mesoamerica lacked the contact with foreign people, ideas, institutions. It moved without changing: a perpetual return to the point of departure. All civilizations—including China and Japan—have been the result of intersections and clashes with foreign cultures. All, except the pre-Hispanic civilizations of America. The ancient Mexicans saw the Spanish as supernatural beings who had come from another world because they did not have the mental categories in which to place them. They lacked the experience and the concepts that marked the people of other civilizations.*

The foundation of Hindu civilization is Indo-European. The culture that was born in the Indus Valley is more an antecedent than an origin. I am aware that in Mohenjo-daro and Harappa there are prefigurations of Indian culture and religion: a proto-Shiva, the lingam, the cult of the Great Goddess and of tree spirits. Nevertheless, the Indus civilization, of which we know little, seems to me to have more affinities with Mesopotamia. (It is hardly necessary to make clear that, speaking of Indo-Europeans, I allude not to a race, but to realities and concepts that are linguistic, cultural, and historical.) The characteristic features of Hindu civilization are undeniably of Indo-European origin: the Vedas and the other sacred writings, the mythology, the sacred and literary language, the great poems, and, most of all, the social organization. Once again, I must cite Georges Dumézil, who has demonstrated the relation between Indian mythology and that of the other Indo-European peoples (Celts, Iranians, Germans, Romans, Greeks), the Indo-European origin of the caste sys-

* See my essays "Asia y América" in *Puertas al campo* (untranslated in English); "The Art of Mexico: Material and Substance" in *Essays on Mexican Art*; and "The Eagle, the Jaguar, and the Virgin," the introduction to *Mexico: Thirty Centuries of Splendor*, a catalog of the exhibition presented in 1990 by the Metropolitan Museum of Art in New York City.

tem, and, above all, the dominance of the tripartite vision of the world, whether in the myths or in the three social categories: priests, warriors, and artisans.

Communities with the same linguistic and cultural origins do not necessarily evolve in the same ways. The development of Indian civilization may be seen as a case of reverse symmetry to that of the West.* There is nothing in the history of ancient India comparable in significance and consequences to the diffusion of Hellenism or the imperial rule of Rome. Hellenism unified the elites of the Mediterranean peoples and of the ancient civilizations of the Near and Middle East; Rome completed the work of Alexander and his successors, transforming a cultural universalism—philosophy and science, arts and literature—into a political, economic, and administrative reality. The influence was reciprocal: Rome unified the world, and the elites adopted Greco-Roman culture and thought; the peoples subservient to Roman political institutions in turn influenced their conquerors, particularly in religion. Rome and Alexandria erected altars to Isis and Serapis, Atthis and Cybele, Astarte and Mithra. In India, to the contrary, the process of unification of the various peoples and cultures of the subcontinent was the work not of an imperial state, or of a predominantly philosophical and literary culture such as the Greek, but of the religious expansion of Hinduism and Buddhism. The state was the central protagonist of Mediterranean antiquity: kings, caesars, consuls, generals, orators, administrators; in India, the historical agents were the religious reformers and their adepts and disciples, religious bodies, sects, and monks, almost always allied with the power

---

* I have explored this contradictory symmetry in artistic styles and in the religious attitudes toward the body in *Conjunctions and Disjunctions*, translated by Helen Lane, Viking Press, New York, 1974.

of a dynasty, a caste, or a group like the urban merchants who protected Buddhism. In one case, the supremacy of the political; in the other, of the religious.

The great absence in classical India was a universal state. It is the central fact, the one that has determined Indian history to the present day. The three great historical empires—the Maurya, Gupta, and Mughal—never ruled the entire subcontinent. The political history of India was always that of rival monarchies in perennial conflict with one another. Only since the nineteenth century, with the British Empire, has India been governed by a central power that has jurisdiction over all its inhabitants. The present state, in certain fundamental aspects—universal sovereignty, democracy, the party system, equality before the law, human rights, and freedom of religion—is the legacy of the British Raj. Something similar may be said of Mexico, although the Spanish legacy did not include the modern principles I have mentioned. We are the children of the Counter-Reformation. In Mexico, the reality as well as the idea of being a nation had already been born in the seventeenth century, a hundred years after the Conquest. Before the arrival of the Spanish conquistadors, the peoples of Mesoamerica, like those of India, shared a civilization with common values, but they lived in permanent war with one another. The Spanish domination ended that war and unified the various nations under one state. The present Mexican state is the heir of the Spanish state and not, as has often been said, of the Aztec. The Aztecs never ruled other nations, nor did they attempt it. For them, war had an economic function (the tribute of the conquered) and a religious one (human sacrifice).

In Europe, the domination by Rome prepared the way for the other great event in the history of the West, one that also has no equivalent in India: the triumph of Christian mono-theism. At the fall of the Roman Empire, the Church took its place. In this way Europe avoided a return to barbarity and maintained its ties with Greco-Roman antiquity. The barbar-ians became Christians; in turn, Christianity recognized the Greco-Roman legacy. In the Eastern Empire, Christianity became identified with the Byzantine state; in the West, Latin became the language of religion, philosophy, and culture. Thus Christian monotheism radically changed the pagan so-cieties without breaking completely with the ancient civ-ilization. In India nothing similar occurred. The original Brahmanic religion underwent many changes, of which one was decisive: Buddhism. In turn, Buddhism went through a period of stagnancy that coincided first with the reemergence of Brahmanic influence and then with the appearance of Islam on the subcontinent. Buddhism disappeared from India—an immense loss. And, of course, the relations between Hinduism and Islam were not mutually rewarding: they lived beside each other in continual hostility. In Europe, first the Church fathers and later the great medieval scholars were nourished by Greek philosophy. Virgil guided Dante on his journey through the Inferno. In contrast, the Muslim theologians did not look on the Vedas or the Upanishads with the same veneration with which St. Augustine or St. Thomas Aquinas studied Plato or Aristotle.

Monotheism arrived too late in India, and in one of its most radical and extreme versions: Islam. I am referring to monotheism as a religion: the concept of a single principle appears equally among the Greek philosophers and the Indian, as one can see in the speculations of a Plotinus or a Shankara, to take only two examples. But philosophical deism is one thing, and monotheism in its three great manifestations—

Christian, Jewish, Islamic—something else entirely. One need not share Freud's theory that the origin of Jewish monotheism was the theological absolutism of the pharaoh Akhenaton (Amenophis IV) to understand the natural relation between a single power and the belief in a single god. This has been the great strength of monotheism: its ability to be transformed into the soul of an international state, as is seen in the cases of the Byzantine Empire and the Caliphate. Monotheism has been the great unifier of different peoples, languages, races, and cultures. It has also been a great divider of people and the source of endless and terrible intolerance. The relative disaster of Islam in India—it tried to convert millions, but the majority remained faithful to their old beliefs and gods—is proof of the double face of monotheism: when it does not unite, it tears apart.

India owes to Islam admirable works of architecture, painting, music, and landscaping, not to mention its great historical achievements, like the creation of the Mughal Empire. Nevertheless, the coexistence of Islam and Hinduism has been, except in rare moments, a rivalry that has often turned into violence. I have referred to the example of Christian monotheism which achieved both the religious unification of Europe and the continuation of the ancient Greco-Roman civilization. This was possible because the Church fathers, as well as the later scholars, grafted Greek philosophy onto Christian doctrine. Without Plato, Aristotle, Seneca, and the Stoics, the Christians would probably have had no philosophy. Thus, from the first centuries to the present time, Greco-Roman culture has never ceased to enrich us. Greek philosophy also had a profound influence on Islam: it was, after all, the Arabs who transmitted the thought of Aristotle and the medicine of Galen to medieval Europe. Yet Greek thought vanished from Islam without fundamentally changing it. Averroës failed, while Thomas Aquinas triumphed. Perhaps this is why neither Islamic nor Hindu civilization experienced anything comparable to the Renaissance. Here is the third singularity of Hindu civilization, which it shares with Islam: neither of the two had a religious Reformation or a cultural, artistic, and philosophical Renaissance. These two movements are the basis of modernity, and without them the European expansion, begun by the Portuguese and Spanish in the sixteenth century, would have been arrested. At the moment of their great imperialist expansion, the Europeans encountered petrified cultures.

The contrary and complementary example is that of the American peoples, who could not resist the European invaders; their cultures disappeared, the opposite of what occurred with the Hindus, Muslims, and Chinese under European imperialism. The clash between the Europeans and the Mesoamericans was a violent encounter between civilizations that resulted in the destruction of a magical mentality and a ritualistic culture. The scientific, philosophical, technological, and political inferiority of the Mesoamericans does not entirely explain the Conquest. There was also a political-religious fact that favored the Spanish: Mesoamerica was a perpetual battleground. The central idea of the Mesoamericans, from the Mayas and the Zapotecs to the Aztecs and the Teotihuacanians, was the sacred character of war. The world had been created by a cosmic war between celestial gods and by divine sacrifice: the blood of the gods had given birth to the world. The battles between men were recurrent and ritualistic repetitions of the cosmic war, and they ended with the sacrifice of the conquered warriors at the top of a pyramid. The meaning of the sacrifice becomes clearer when we consider its double function: on the one hand, to nourish the gods with the divine food, blood, and therefore aid in the perpetuation of the cosmic order; on the other, to divinize the victim. I have already mentioned another factor that is rarely discussed by scholars: the historical solitude. The encounter with the Europeans proved fatal for those nations because their isolation, which had preserved them from the outside world, had also disarmed them against any outside influence. In less than a century all the pre-Hispanic societies—except for a few isolated tribes protected by the jungle, the desert, or other natural barriers—were dominated by the Spanish. In some regions epidemics—another disastrous consequence of isolation—decimated the population.

The clash of civilizations was, as nearly always in history, a battle between two visions of this world and the other world, that is to say, two religions. As in India, the conflict in the New World was between the polytheism of the natives and the monotheism of the invaders. But, unlike India, it led not to coexistence but to the destruction of the ancient polytheism and the mass conversion to Christian monotheism. This conversion, like all conversions, was both voluntary and forced. Voluntary because the new religion offered the Mesoamericans freedom from the terrible oppressions of the old cults and the blood-soaked institutions of permanent war and sacrifice. Forced because Christianity was a religion imposed by the conquerors. I cannot and need not dwell at length on this topic. I should, however, mention in passing a circumstance that explains the conversion of the Mexicans. It is not a complete explanation—no historical explanation is—but without it the phenomenon becomes an insoluble enigma. I have said that one belief united all these peoples: cosmic war and the sacrifice. The gods battled and sacrificed themselves to create the world (or, more exactly, to re-create it, since the myths speak of previous worlds). Thus the idea of sacrifice is the heart, literally and figuratively, of the Mesoamerican religions. Blood, like rain, is life-giving. Christianity offered them a sublimation of that belief: the sacrifice of a god who became a man and spilled his blood to redeem the world. This idea had scandalized the Greeks and Romans, as later, when they learned of it, it scandalized the Hindus and Chinese: a condemned god, God as victim! But for the Mexicans this idea was a bridge between their ancient religion and Christianity.

The literature on the Spanish and Portuguese domination is full of somber details and harsh judgments. Without denying the veracity of many of these descriptions and criticisms, one must say that it represents a unilateral vision. Many of these denunciations were inspired by the envy and imperialist rivalry among the French, English, and Dutch. Not all was horror: over the ruins of the pre-Columbian world the Spanish and Portuguese raised a grandiose historical construction, much of which is still in place. They united many peoples who spoke different languages, worshiped different gods, fought among themselves, or were ignorant of one another. These peoples became united by laws and judicial institutions, but, above all, by language, culture, and religion. Although the losses were enormous, the gains were immense.

To measure fairly the effect of the Spanish in Mexico, one must emphasize that without them—that is, without the Catholic religion and the culture the Spanish implanted in our country—we would not be what we are. We would probably be a collection of peoples divided by different beliefs, languages, and cultures. Here I must emphasize a circumstance that seems to me essential, and without which it is impossible to explain the transition from polytheism to monotheism. Catholicism was the version of Christianity that was imposed on Mexico. I have mentioned the rediscovery of Greek philosophy, first made by the Church fathers, and later by the medieval scholasticists. No less determining was the transformation of the ancient pagan gods into Christian saints and devils. More than a thousand years later, the same phenomenon was repeated in Mexico. One of the great creations of Mexican Catholicism was the appearance of the Virgin of Guadalupe to a Mexican Indian, on the same hill where, before the Conquest, a pre-Hispanic goddess had been worshiped. Catholicism was able to take root in Mexico by transforming the ancient gods into the saints, virgins, and devils of the new religion. Nothing similar could occur in India with Muslim monotheism or Protestant Christianity, both of which saw the cult of images, of saints and virgins, as idolatry.

Spanish Catholicism has often proved to be intolerant because it has been possessed with the spirit of crusade. It was a religion formed during centuries of struggle against an equally intransigent monotheism: Islam. Nevertheless, as an heir of Rome, it possessed a capacity to assimilate foreign cults which the far more rigid Protestantism lacked. The Spanish and Portuguese were committed to converting the infidels, and did not hesitate at the use of force to achieve that goal. They were the last pre-modern empires. The English never exhibited much interest in Christianizing the people under their domain. And in the places where the imperial state was content merely to administer the conquered nations, as occurred with European imperialism in the modern era, the old tribal and religious quarrels were resumed as soon as those nations gained their independence. The English left an invaluable legacy in India: democratic institutions, the rule of law, and modern administration that the Indians had the talent to maintain. But they also left intact the ancient religious, ethnic, and cultural divisions. Those divisions, which had disappeared under British power, quickly turned into bloody civil struggles. The result was the current tripartition: India, Pakistan, and Bangladesh.

GANDHI: CENTER AND EXTREME

India's first extended contact with Christian monotheism was through the Portuguese, who established a settlement in Goa in 1510.* The Portuguese attempted to extend their domain and convert various groups, but they soon had to compete and wage war with other European powers—the Dutch, French, and English—who were seeking footholds and commercial privileges. India was torn by these struggles among the various empires, a state of anarchy that became most pronounced at the beginning of the eighteenth century, after the death of Aurangzeb. In the end, the British overcame all their foreign and local rivals after a military and diplomatic war that had lasted two centuries, and in 1868 they established the Viceroyalty of India.

British rule was marked by certain characteristics that should be noted. The first is that British imperialism arrived in India accompanied by, but not united with, Protestantism and modernity. Although the British government was

---

* I exclude the legend of St. Thomas's two visits to India. (On the second visit, according to tradition, he was martyred in Mylapore in A.D. 68) It is certain, however, that Christian communities belonging to the Syrian Church were founded on the Malabar Coast in the first century; these still survive. But the version of Christianity presented to the Indians in the sixteenth century was quite different. See Romila Thapar, *History of India*, vol. 1, Penguin, London, 1966.

considered Christian, there was no state religion, and the English state, unlike the Spanish in the Americas, did not attempt the conversion of the native inhabitants. The separation of temporal power and the various Christian churches was, from the beginning, a fact accepted by all. Moreover, the Christians were divided into sects, and could not constitute a power to rival that of the state, as occurred in the Spanish colonies. Nor were there, among the Protestant churches, orders as powerful as those of the Dominicans or, above all, the Jesuits. The christianization of India was an enterprise undertaken by missionaries who belonged to various denominations. The kinds of monotheism they professed made it impossible for them to absorb the images and idols worshiped by Hindus. Nor could they combine and adapt as the Jesuits had done, whether accepting the caste system in the south of India or declaring that Chinese ancestor worship was not heretical. The Christianity imported by the British was a modern version of the religion: separation of church and state, abolition of the cult of images, freedom to interpret the Scriptures, and the other principles of the Reformation. A religion poor in rites and ceremonies, but full of moral and sexual rigidity. In other words: the exact opposite of popular Hinduism.

Modernity begins with the Reformation: one of its essential elements is the freedom of examination, that is to say, criticism. The Christianity that came to India with the British carried within itself the great element that dissolves beliefs: the free interpretation of the Scriptures. With Protestantism came modern thinking: philosophy, science, political democracy, nationalism. Imperialism introduced modernity to India, and with it the criticism of its own regime. In Mexico, the criticism of the abuses of the Spanish was the work of priests, such as Bartolomé de las Casas, whose arguments were based on medieval Christianity and scholastic philosophy. Precisely the opposite occurred in India: there the adoption of modernity, by a handful of intellectuals, implied a criticism of the British rule according to the very principles of the British system.

For commercial as well as political reasons, the representatives of the Company initially used Persian, the official language of the Delhi court, in their dealings with the natives. The English quickly became interested in Indian civilization, and in 1784 the Orientalist William Jones founded the Asiatic Society in Calcutta, then the capital of British India. In turn, many Indians learned English, most of them for practical reasons, but some out of a genuine interest in European culture. Nearly all were Bengali Brahmans, and with them, in the strict sense, modern India begins. It was a renaissance of Hinduism, but of a Hinduism influenced by Protestantism, and it would be the birth of the political movement toward Independence.

British influence would have been limited to a very few had it not been for the introduction of the English system of education. This decision was made in 1835 under the recommendation of Lord Macaulay, then a man of thirty-four, who the year before had been named president of the Commission of Public Instruction. One should add that twelve years earlier, in a letter to the Governor General, Ram Mohan Roy, now known as the "father of modern India," had requested that schools be established in Bengal to teach the natives English rather than Persian or Sanskrit: "I beg your Lordship will be pleased to compare the state of Science and Literature in Europe before the time of Lord Bacon with the progress in knowledge made since he wrote.... [To adopt] the Sanskrit system of education [as, among others, William Jones had proposed] would be best calculated to keep this country in darkness." Roy admired Hindu tradition and never converted to Christianity; his argument cannot be seen as a betrayal. As for Macaulay, he based his decision both on his evident disdain for Hindu and Muslim tradition and on his exalted view of European culture, particularly the English language. He saw English, not unreasonably, as the universal language of the future. Macaulay's contempt for Asian cultures was due to his ignorance of their traditions, a rare error of perspective for a historian of his distinction. Nevertheless, he was essentially right: since the thirteenth century, neither the Hindus nor the Muslims had produced a body of knowledge or of literary and artistic works comparable to that of the Europeans. The two civilizations were petrified spiritually, and in perpetual political and social turmoil.

Macaulay's plan was to open the world of modern culture to the Indians, and in his defense he cited the precedent of Russia: "Within the last hundred and twenty years, a nation, which has previously been in a state as barbarous as that in which our ancestors were before the Crusades, has gradually emerged from the ignorance in which it was sunk, and has taken its place among civilized communities.... The languages of western Europe civilized Russia. I cannot doubt that they will do for the Hindoo what they have done for the Tartar." Macaulay admitted that it was impossible to extend the British system of education to the entire population. This is another difference from Spanish rule in the Americas: the imposition of the Spanish language on the indigenous population had two goals, one political-administrative and the other religious. Neither goal was intended by Macaulay or the British administration. Macaulay, in fact, stated, "It is impossible for us, with our limited means, to attempt to educate the body of the people. We must at present do our best to form a class who may be interpreters between us and the millions whom we govern; a class of persons, Indian in blood and color, but English in tastes, opinions, morals, and in intellect." This class, he added, would gradually extend modern knowledge to the great mass of the population.

Macaulay's proposal was a success. The education reforms of 1835 had consequences that were decisive in the formation of modern India and that continue to influence life in the country. First, the reforms created, as Macaulay intended, a class of Anglophilic Indians, first in Bengal and later in the principal urban centers, such as Bombay, Delhi, and Madras. But this class soon took the English and European ideas and used them to reinterpret their own traditions, thus sowing the seeds of the independence movement. Second, they provided India with a universal language. Today, as I have noted, English continues to be the language of communication among the diverse linguistic communities. But the reforms disunited as well as united. Persian was replaced as the official language, and the Muslim community felt itself similarly replaced. They sealed themselves off in their traditions, which put them at a disadvantage compared to the Hindus. Later, they jealously imitated their rivals and trained themselves in the new ways of speaking and thinking, but the split between the two communities had already become wider and deeper. The participation in British culture, common to both, had separated rather than united the Hindus and Muslims, perhaps because their respective interpretations of modern culture did not entail an abandonment of their religions. It would take two generations before there were truly secular and agnostic figures, such as Nehru. Indian intellectuals saw modern European culture not as a universal critical way of thinking, but as a way to purify their traditions, which had been deformed by centuries of ignorance, intellectual stagnancy, and millennarian superstition.*

The political movement was preceded by a reform of Hinduism in which the influence of English Christianity was decisive. The leader of this reformation, Ram Mohan Roy, attempted to restore Hinduism to its original purity. Influenced by the ideas of the Unitarian church, he found proof in the sacred texts of Brahmanism that the true Hindu religion, now deformed by superstition, was a monotheism no less rigorous than that of the Christians. Ignoring the differences, he sought out the ways in which Indian and Western thought resemble one another. I am certain that he never realized that he was the creator of a pious fraud. The same confusion may be seen in the reformers who followed him. The well-known Sri Ramakrishna preached a return to traditional religion; he was a devotee of the Great Goddess and often beheld her in his visions. He also "saw God in His various manifestations: Krishna, Christ, Muhammad [sic]." Ramakrishna's disciple, Swami Vivekananda, in a speech given in 1899, lamented the weakness of the Hindus, who had unconsciously accepted Western customs. He urged them to return to the ancient rites and beliefs: Hindus should "embrace one another like true brothers," without caste distinctions. Apart from his evangelical zeal, this exhortation contained a triple heresy: an embrace between different caste members (a contamination), brotherhood among men (a denial of karmic law), and the postulation of the existence of a creator God. To defend Hinduism against the criticism of the

---

* See, on this subject and others below, the section "Modern India and Pakistan," edited by Stephen N. Hay, in *Sources of the Indian Tradition*, vol. II, Columbia University Press, New York, 1960, an anthology of documents on the reformers and their successors, with useful introductory notes.

missionaries, the reformers Christianized it. Their secret religion was Christianity; without knowing or wanting to, they had adopted its values.

The rediscovery of Hinduism by these Anglophilic Brahmans and intellectuals, beyond the rigor and exactitude of their interpretations of the Vedas and other sacred texts, led them to discover that they were the heirs of a great civilization. At the same time, many spiritually discontented Europeans, the unhappy children of modernity, discovered in the Asian doctrines a previously unknown fountain of wisdom. The Theosophical Society, which was quite influential in those years, adopted the Hindu doctrine of metempsychosis and karmic law. Annie Besant, well known for her part in the history of Fabian socialism, joined the Society and presided over it until her death in 1933. At the beginning of the century she settled in India, participated in the struggle for independence, was imprisoned, and in 1917 was elected president of the Indian National Congress. She was the fifth—and last—British citizen to hold that post.*

The nationalist tendencies were nourished by the ideas of the religious reformers. And not only their ideas but also their sentiments and passions. Hinduism and nationalism became synonymous. Something similar occurred among the Muslims: a parallel movement preached the cleansing of superstitions and foreign beliefs. In reality, it was attempting to varnish Islam with Christianity. For the Muslims, too, politics became indistinguishable from religion (if Islam has ever made this distinction). It was therefore not unexpected that the Muslims looked with suspicion upon the activities of the Indian

---

* Besant believed that in one of her previous existences she had been a Hindu. She had also been Hippatia and Giordano Bruno.

National Congress. From its beginning, the differences between the Muslims and Hindus had stained the Congress with religious passion and intolerance. The struggle for independence was often a struggle against the religious enemy. The Indian National Congress gathered for the first time in 1885; Allan O. Hume, a Scot of generally moderate tendencies, was instrumental in its formation. The Congress was a sort of loyal opposition to the colonial administration; only much later, through the work of Gandhi, did it change its methods and objectives. The Muslims barely participated in these activities.

Shortly after its founding, the Congress divided into moderates and extremists. The former, ardent admirers of the English democratic system, were gradualists who recognized that institutions change more slowly than laws: English democracy was the result of the evolution of that society since the sixteenth century. But English democracy was one thing in England and another in India; the moderates tended to ignore the abuses committed by many of the British colonialists, who were steeped in the idea of their superiority to the natives. Moreover, in their relations with the Viceregal government, the moderates were often overly cautious. Nevertheless, they were the ones who secured the rights of freedom of expression and association that were later used by the extremists. The moderates belonged to the most affluent groups of the society and stood to gain from far-reaching reforms in economics and social relations. In this sense they were the precursors of modern India. Their perspective was secular and, although many of them were believers, they always carefully separated the matters of this world from those of the other. Most valuable of all, they were democrats. But these attitudes, in themselves commendable, caused the moderates to be alienated from the populist groups, who were moved by religious passions.

The extremists quickly won over the masses with their intransigence toward the foreign power, their demands for social justice, and their frenetic nationalism not only against the British authorities but also against the religious and ethnic minorities, particularly the Muslims. They carried verbal violence into action: angry demonstrations, riots, and, in some cases, terrorist attacks. Some of their leaders were sent to prison and thus turned into popular heroes. The success of the extremist tactics was essentially due to their union of two populist passions: religion and nationalism. The Hindus were profoundly religious, but their religiosity had become more active and aggressive with the injection of a new passion, nationalism, hitherto unknown in India or Asia. Nationalist ideology is a modern European invention, and its combination with traditional religions has proved to be explosive. The Hindu nationalism of Congress extremists like B. G. Tilak (1856–1920) was the seed of the ideology of the current Bharatiya Janata Party (BJP), which now threatens not only democracy but the unity of India itself.*

The extremists' passion was not solely directed against the

---

* The BJP is a nationalist party whose goal is to convert India into a Hindu nation. Its most violent elements were responsible for the destruction of a mosque in the small city of Ayodhya in the state of Uttar Pradesh in the north of India, the supposed birthplace of the god Rāma, an avatar of Vishnu. According to the nationalists, in 1528 the emperor Babur leveled a temple dedicated to Rāma and built a mosque on the ruins. On December 6, 1992, a mob of 300,000 fanatics, brought together by the party and other extreme right-wing groups, destroyed the mosque and quickly built a shrine dedicated to Rāma. The result was a series of riots, especially in Bombay, in which more than 1,500 people, largely Muslims, died. Previously the major opposition party in Parliament, the BJP won a plurality of seats in the 1996 national elections but were unable to form a government. The country is currently led by a center-left coalition.

British. Tilak was a native of Maharashtra, which since the seventeenth century had been the center of the revolt against the Mughals. Tilak decided to celebrate two festivals in the Maratha region, one in honor of the elephant god Ganesha and the other in memory of Shivājī, the Maratha hero who fought against Aurangzeb. It was a revival of the traditional struggle against Islam: the date of the celebration of Ganesha coincided with that of a Muslim religious festival. The union of politics and religion, nationalism and Hinduism, could not have been more complete. And yet, in the attitude of Tilak and the other extremists there was a contradiction that continues today among the Hinduists of the BJP and other ultra-right groups (although they never mention it): the idea of a nation is incompatible with the institution of caste. Hindu nationalism turns all the social groups into a more or less homogeneous whole: a nation. The castes disappear, or are turned into realities that are subordinate to the reality of realities, the Hindu nation. The foundation of this nationalism is religious, but the existence of castes is one of the consequences of karmic law, the central principle of Hinduism. Neither the extremists in the past nor the present-day nationalists have confronted this contradiction, but the fact that they haven't does not mean that it does not exist. Its significance is clear: Hindu nationalism, like the other political-religious so-called fundamentalisms—for example, in the Middle East and North Africa—is a reactionary version of a modern ideology. The great failure of the Nazis was that they could not invoke an Odin or a Thor as the Hindus have enlisted Rāma in their ranks, or the Muslims Muhammad.

The split between moderates and extremists paralyzed the Congress. Neither of the two groups was able to carry out successfully the movement for independence. At that moment, in 1920, Mohandas K. Gandhi became the central figure. In the same year, like a sign of new times, Tilak died. Gandhi's actions, both religious and political—which, in his case, cannot be separated—not only resolved a situation that had seemed hopeless; he turned it into a triumph. The extremists also united the religious and the political, but with Gandhi the point of the union was quite different: nonviolence and friendship with the other religious communities, particularly the Muslims. Contrary to the extremists, for Gandhi politics did not expropriate religion: religion humanized politics. The Gandhian religion was not that of the orthodoxy; it was a reform version acceptable to the masses because they approved of his personal conduct. Gandhi achieved what the moderates could not: establishing deep roots among the people, and at the same time demonstrating to the extremists that tolerance and nonviolence were not incompatible with perseverance and effectiveness. For the masses, Gandhi embodied a figure venerated by all Hindus: the ascetic who renounces the world; for political and practical minds, he was a man of action, capable of speaking both to the masses and with the authorities, skilled in negotiation and incorruptible in his principles.

This fusion of the religious and the political, of asceticism and pragmatism, is only one aspect of the startling concordance of contradictions that made Gandhi a unique figure. He was a traditional Hindu but also a Westerner. The influence of the West was profound and is clearly perceptible in his political thinking and in his religion, the two inseparable sides of his personality. His political actions were not founded on any Hindu tradition, but rather on the pacifism of Leo Tolstoy; his ideas of social reform are closer to Kropotkin than to the Laws of Manu; behind his idea of passive resistance lies

Thoreau's "civil disobedience." His family was Vishnuite, and he himself was an ardent devotee of Vishnu, yet he read the *Bhagavad-Gītā* in the English translation by Sir Edwin Arnold. In Gandhi, the Jain tradition of nonviolence (*ahimsā*) was fused with the activism of a Tolstoy or a Thoreau. (In 1847, Thoreau went to jail rather than pay the taxes for the American war against Mexico.) Nonviolence in India has a double basis: one, political and ethical, which is Western; the other, religious, which is Jain. I should emphasize that Jainism, although it has been integrated into the Hindu tradition, has always been viewed by the orthodox as a tendency that does not belong in the pluralism of Hinduism.

Jain cosmology affirms the solidarity of all living things: to commit an act of violence against one creature, no matter how small, is to sin against the entire cosmos. I remember my astonishment when I saw a group of Jain monks—who have, by the way, prodigious memories—with their mouths covered by a piece of cloth so as not to inhale, and inadvertently kill, any insects. The "gymnosophist" (that is, naked) philosophers who amazed Alexander and his retinue with the subtlety of their reasoning and the rigor of their austerities were probably Jains.

Many prosperous jewelers and merchants in India are also Jain. In spite of their tenet of nonviolence, writes A. L. Basham, "Jain ethical writings often have a rather chilly character, their altruism motivated by a higher selfishness." Jain pragmatism is perceptible in Gandhi, though without the frigidity. His genius consisted in transforming the nonviolence of personal religious morals into a collective crusade that inspired millions. Although the Congress Party was always a secular movement, it was subject to various religious influences, all of them Hindu. This was its great failure: it never could attract a sufficient number of Muslims. Here too, although he was not successful, Gandhi was an exception: he stretched out his hand to the Muslims and Sikhs. Religion did not impede his pragmatic and realistic politics; politics, in turn, did not stain or confuse his faith.

His doctrine was contradictory: he was a nationalist who believed in democracy yet at the same time hated Western technology and industry. He considered Western civilization a "disease." "I am not the enemy of the English; I am the enemy of their civilization." (*Hind Swarāj*, Indian Home Rule, 1909). He saw the railroad and the telegraph as disastrous inventions...but he used them. His social utopia was an idealization of ancient Hindu civilization that had no more reality than Rousseau's natural man. His teachings had a double and contradictory objective: to free the Indian people from British domination and to return to a peaceful society, outside of time, dedicated to agriculture, opposed to material gain, and believing in traditional religion. An Arcadia populated not by love-sick shepherds but by ascetics in love with their gods, who were all manifestations or incarnations of Truth. Gandhi never wanted to—or was unable to—explain to his listeners and readers what exactly that Truth was that inspired his words and deeds. But one does not look to him for logic or philosophical coherence. He was not Socrates, and the secret of his immense influence over his people does not lie in his reasoning, but rather in the union of act and word in the service of a disinterested ideal. He wanted neither power nor glory: he sought to serve others, particularly the unfortunate. He proved it with his life and with his death.

In an impious century such as ours, the figure of Gandhi is almost a miracle. Within him, opposites merged: action and passivity, politics—the most naked form of the appetite for power—at the service of a religion of disinterest. A living contradiction: he always affirmed his belief in traditional religion, and yet there is nothing more remote from orthodox Hinduism than fraternization among the castes, friendship with Muslims, and the doctrine of nonviolence. It is not easy to agree—and I do not—with many of Gandhi's political and philosophical ideas. I understand and share his horror of many aspects of contemporary technological civilization, but the solutions he proposed were at times unrealistic, at times positively harmful. Poverty is not a solution to injustice or excess. But we ought not to judge him. Saints are not judged, they are venerated.

The assassination of Gandhi cannot be seen merely as a political crime: his assassin and the group that inspired him did not view Gandhi as a political adversary but as a heretic. For the Hindu nationalists, heirs of the hatred that Tilak expressed toward Islam, the heresies of Gandhi, which they never ceased to denounce—for example, his blasphemous interpretation of the *Gītā,* which does not condemn violence but exalts it as the *dharma* of the warrior—had culminated in an abomination. Not only had he been incapable of avoiding the secession of Pakistan, but he had begun a hunger strike in an attempt to end the massacres and to persuade the Hindu mobs to leave the mosques they had invaded in Delhi and other places. In 1938, Gandhi had declared: "My Hinduism is not sectarian. It includes the best, in my opinion, of Islam, Christianity, Buddhism, and Zoroastrianism. . . . All my life I have worked for the unity of Hindus and Muslims. It has been the passion of my early youth. Among my best and most noble friends are some who are Muslim."

Gandhi's assassin, N. V. Godse, was a close associate and lieutenant of V. D. Savarkar, a Brahman preacher who, like

Tilak, was from Maharashtra. An ardent nationalist, Savarkar was noted early on for the violence of his ideas and actions. He lived in London between 1906 and 1910, outwardly a law student, but in fact dedicated to terrorist activities. There he polemicized with Gandhi, in 1909. Pursued by the British police, he attempted unsuccessfully to seek asylum in France. Condemned in 1911 to life imprisonment in a penal colony on the Andaman Islands, he was released in 1924 on the condition that he not participate in political activities. Nevertheless, in 1937 he publicly resumed his political career at the head of the Hindu Mahasabha (Great Assembly of Hindus) Party. Seven years later, he had to resign for reasons of health. Although Savarkar was intellectually responsible for the assassination of Gandhi, his complicity in the crime could never be proven, and he was released for lack of evidence.

Savarkar's ideas have been the theoretical source of all the Hindu nationalist movements, and today they are the heart of the doctrines of the Bharatiya Janata Party. One of his books, *Hindutva,* a compendium of his ideas, has become a classic for the Hindu nationalists. The title is difficult to translate; like *négritude* or *hispanidad,* it means something like "Hinduicity": that which is characteristic and essential to Hindu being. For Savarkar, "to be Hindu means a person who sees this land, from the Indus River to the sea, as his country but also as his Holy Land."* Savarkar combines two distinct notions: one territorial and one religious. For example, he "advocated the removal of intercaste barriers, the entry of Untouchables into the orthodox temples, and the reconversion of Hindus who

---

* On the contemporary nationalist movement, see the trenchant essay by Ashutosh Varsheney, "Battling the Past, Forging a Future? Ayodhya and Beyond" in *India Briefings,* a collection of articles edited by Phillip Oldenberg and published by the Asia Society in 1993.

had become Muslims or Christians."* In this, Hindu nationalism may be seen as somewhat similar to the ideas of Gandhi, in that it implies a reform, however limited, of religion. The difference, which is essential, is that the Hinduism of Gandhi was inclusive and understood other religions and ways of thinking, while that of Savarkar was exclusive: to be an Indian it is not enough to have been born in India, one must be part of Hindu culture. The image the nationalists have of Indian culture is a mutilated one; in it there is no place for Akbar or the poet Amir Khushrau, the Red Fort in Delhi or the Taj Mahal in Agra, not to mention the Sikhs or the great Buddhist philosophers. India, as a culture and as a history, is far greater than Hinduism, and thus Hindu nationalism lives in a permanent contradiction: its idea of Indian culture is religious; its vision of the Hindu religion entails its transformation into a political belief. The conversion of a culture into a religion ends with the conversion of a religion into politics.

Like all nationalisms, the Hindu version is a political religion. That is, a political corruption of religion. In the Islamic tradition this confusion has been recurrent, and it is one of the negative aspects of the history of Arab civilization. The three great monotheisms have lent themselves with greater ease to this kind of combination: one God, one law, and one ruler. Hindu nationalism has fallen into a kind of caricature of monotheism by replacing its original pluralism and polytheism with the adoration of a single ideological god: the nation. There is more than a similarity between Hindu and Islamic nationalism. The basis of the latter is religious and is in the Qur'an. Therefore a critique of Islamic nationalism, whether in Pakistan or in the other Muslim nations, must

---

* Stephen N. Hay, *Sources of the Indian Tradition*.

begin as a critique of the Sharī'a (the Sunnite orthodoxy) to determine what is alive and permanent in it, and what is circumstantial, plainly political.* The problems are similar for a Hindu intellectual. Both critiques require an enormous enterprise that must be must undertaken in historical circumstances that are particularly unfavorable, not only because of the rebirth of religious and nationalist fanaticism throughout the world, but also because of the absence of a modern critical tradition in their respective cultures. Neither Hinduism nor Islam had a Renaissance, as in Europe, and thus they had no Enlightenment.

I must emphasize that the absence of modern critical thinking does not imply the absence of a great literature. Rabindranath Tagore is one example. He was not a thinker; he was a great artist. His life and work were a bridge between India and the world. Admired by the best in Europe, like W. B. Yeats and André Gide, he also had many ardent readers in the Hispanic world. He visited Buenos Aires and was a friend of Victoria Ocampo, to whom he dedicated a book of his poems. A great poet, Juan Ramón Jiménez, in collaboration with his wife, Zenobia Camprubí, translated much of Tagore's work. Those translations influenced many young poets at the time, among them Pablo Neruda. In one of Neruda's first books, *Twenty Poems of Love and a Song of Despair,* there is an echo, at certain moments, of Tagore's voice. Although he never actively participated in politics, Tagore was a passionate defender of the independence of India and of its values. (His father, Debendranath Tagore, was one of the central figures in the Bengal renaissance of Indian culture.) Between

---

* See the penetrating reflections of Akeel Bilgrami, "What is a Muslim? Fundamental Commitment and Cultural Identity," in *Critical Inquiry,* Summer 1992, University of Chicago Press.

Gandhi and Tagore there were some difficulties, due to the poet's criticism of certain aspects of Gandhian politics, such as the total condemnation of Western civilization and the burning of clothes and other foreign products. (I would prefer, said Tagore, to give those clothes to those who are naked.)

These differences did not profoundly affect the mutual admiration Gandhi and Tagore felt for each another. But it is useful to remember that poets, despite their reputation to the contrary, have generally shown good sense—something one cannot say of saints. Dialogue between a poet and a saint is difficult because a poet, before speaking, must hear others—that is to say, the language, which belongs to everyone and to no one. A saint speaks with God or with himself, two forms of silence.

NATIONALISM, SECULARISM, DEMOCRACY

The Congress Party was always pluralistic, even in its most combative phase. Alongside a religious figure like Gandhi were agnostics like Nehru and nationalists like Subhas Chandra Bose. Bose was extremely popular, as Tilak had been. He was inspired by traditional Hinduism, but, like the extremists in the previous generation, he injected the explosive element of nationalism into it. Bose represented the most aggressive and militant wing of the Congress Party. His virulence brought him close to Fascism, and during the Second World War he fought on the side of the Japanese. He died in Taiwan, in an airplane accident. Although excluded from the official pantheon of the Republic, his memory is venerated by many; at festivals and other popular gatherings, one sees his photograph in the stalls where knickknacks and images of movie stars and the gods are sold.

None of these revolutionaries had direct contact with the international socialist movements. The exception was M. N. Roy, another Brahman from Bengal. His real name was Narendranat Bhattacharya (1887–1954). Although he is little known in Mexico, one period of his life was connected to our political history. Roy joined the nationalist extremists quite young; pursued by the British police, he escaped to Chicago. Later, when the United States entered the First World War, he sought asylum in Mexico, along with many American pacifists and socialists. Those were the years of the Mexican Revolution, and Roy did not take long to associate himself with the most radical groups. He was instrumental in the founding of the Communist Party in Mexico. Impressed by his activities and skills, Lenin—through Mikhail Borodin, the Communist agent in Mexico—invited him to participate in the Third International. Roy traveled to Moscow on an official passport issued by the government of President Carranza and was protected by the Mexican consuls in various countries. He worked as an agent of the Communist International in Central Asia and China, but broke with the Comintern in 1929 and finally, some years later, with Marxism itself. He returned to India, fought for independence, and spent years in prison. During the Second World War, understanding the threat posed by the Nazis and the Japanese, he supported collaboration with England and the other democratic nations—the opposite of Gandhi and Nehru's policy of noncooperation. Convinced that the totalitarian system founded by Lenin and the Bolsheviks was a disaster, he invented a revolutionary response to the crisis of socialism: "radical humanism." His answer was inadequate, but the motives that inspired it were legitimate. The life and work of Roy are an example of the fate of the revolutionary intellectual in the twentieth century.*

With a figure like Jawaharlal Nehru, who declared himself a socialist but was the leader of a nationalist movement like the Congress Party, it is legitimate to ask what his true ideology was. He was a socialist if one considers his earliest political activities, his efforts to steer the Congress Party toward the left, his differences with Gandhi and Sardar V. Patel, and his public declarations and pronouncements. Yet despite the intense interest with which he followed international politics, his activities all took place in India and were dedicated to independence from British rule. In the beginning, his rationalism and socialism were at odds with Gandhi, despite his admiration for a man who had been able to mobilize millions in a pacifist crusade. But he was disturbed by the fact that these political actions were propelled by a religious spirit. He understood, however, the effectiveness of this method, and worked with the Mahatma. Finally, thanks to his intelligence and his influence on the militants, he became Gandhi's lieutenant, without sacrificing his political and intellectual independence.

Once Nehru was in power, his socialism did not lead him to take genuinely revolutionary measures, such as the social-

---

* After his death, a book entitled *M. N. Roy's Memoirs* was published (Allied Publishers, Bombay, 1964). A large part of the first section of the book deals with Roy's years in Mexico, which were his revolutionary initiation. The story of the intrigues and complicity between the Carranza government and the German Embassy during the war corroborates what is well known: the efforts by Germany to use Mexico as a base against the United States and Carranza's generally favorable attitude toward this attempt. Unfortunately, it is very difficult to identify the Mexican protagonists in Roy's story: none of the names correspond to known figures. Are these lapses in the author's memory or ignorance on the part of the editors? I mention this because, apart from the names, Roy's descriptions of Mexico City and life in those years are vivid and exact.

ization of property. He did, however, attempt a vigorous policy of economic intervention by the state. He once said that his goal was not the expropriation of capital, but rather its social control. This policy was met with approval by the big Indian capitalists, both for its nationalism (protecting them from foreign competition) and because it was designed to create an economic structure that they themselves could not have built. Something similar occurred in Mexico after the Revolution. Nehru's statism was necessary at the time, as was the Mexican. Later, continued by his successors, it had the results that are typical for this policy throughout the world: patrimonialism, corruption, economic stagnation due to the absence of competition, and the unchecked growth of a bureaucracy motivated by political interests rather than economic logic. The direct beneficiaries of economic statism are not the workers but the bureaucrats.

Nehru's international politics had a brilliant beginning but soon revealed itself to be unilateral and unrealistic. His grand scheme, the creation of a block of nonaligned nations, ended up serving the interests of the Soviet Union more than world peace. Besides the fact that his major allies—Tito, Nasser, Sukarno—were not really democrats, Nehru also developed an imprudent and naive policy of friendship with Mao's regime. He could not—or did not want to—see the schism that divided the Communist powers, and his blindness eventually made him a victim of that split. The humiliating Chinese invasion of India's northwestern frontier, the so-called McMahon Line, was in fact a belligerent warning by Peking directed at Moscow, but through New Delhi. For years Nehru had believed in the friendship of the Chinese, but now he saw them allied with Pakistan. In the subsequent public commotion, he had to disassociate himself from Krishna

Menon, his spokesman at the United Nations and other fo-
rums, whom he had appointed minister of defense. Menon
was an arrogant and intelligent man, but, as so often happens
with the proud, he was not the master of his own ideas: he
was possessed by them. Nehru was never able to recuperate
from this disaster of his foreign policy, and the humiliation
overshadowed his final years.

India's relations with Pakistan have always been bitter,
whether under Nehru or his successors. The dispute over
Kashmir has never ceased to poison minds. The majority of
the state's population is Muslim, and at one point there
seemed to be a compromise solution: to grant Kashmir a degree of economic and political autonomy under the leadership
of Sheik Abdullah, an old friend of Nehru's and an enemy of
the Pakistani regime. But Nehru refused to meet these demands, and went so far as to imprison Abdullah—an unjust
and unpolitical decision. Perhaps he feared that this concession
would inspire other regions to demand the same. Secession is
the permanent threat in India.

Here I must refer briefly to the first and most serious secession, that of Pakistan, which not only cost Gandhi his life,
but also the lives of hundreds of thousands of Hindus and
Muslims.* According to Percival Spear, the blame must be
placed as much on the colonial administration as on the intransigence of Nehru, supported by Gandhi. With the erup-
tion of the Second World War, India, as part of the British
Empire, automatically became a belligerent nation. Furthermore, when the conflict began, many Indians were serving in
the government as elected officials. The majority belonged to

---

* The exact number is unknown, but it is believed to be about a half-million dead. See
Percival Spear, *A History of India,* vol. 2, Penguin Books, New York, 1984.

the Congress Party, which had won decisively with huge margins in the elections. It was an important step toward independence. But the British authorities did not have the wisdom or the tact to consult either the general population or the Congress leadership. The Congress demanded a formal declaration that Great Britain was committed to granting independence to India as one more nation in the Commonwealth. The response from London was vague, and Nehru and his group thought that it was a trick. Gandhi wavered for an instant, but in the end agreed with Nehru, and Congress decided on its policy of non-cooperation, with Gandhi tempering its application. It was not enough and it came too late. The rupture had already occurred, and many Congress members were sent to jail. For its part, the Muslim League, led by the skillful and competent Muhammed Ali Jinnah, used the occasion to expand, and, with the approval of the colonial government, extend its influence among the Muslims. Thus the way was opened for the Partition.

By the time the negotiations began in 1947, Jinnah had become inflexible and demanded the creation of an independent state, Pakistan (the Land of the Pure). Riots broke out throughout the country, particularly in the north, leading to the massacres of Hindus and Muslims that would only be ended by the assassination of Gandhi in January 1948. The split was inevitable. But all these incidents, some terrible and some the product of torpor and intransigence, created the efficient cause, as the scholastics used to say, of the Partition. The deeper reasons are more ancient and are inextricable from the history of India since the thirteenth century. Nehru once compared India to a palimpsest, in which, "one under the other, are written many facts, ideas, and dreams, without any of them completely covering that which is below." The massacres of 1947 did not cover over, they made more visible, the tragic history of the relations between Hindus and Muslims.

Whether among the precursors in Bengal at the turn of the century or among certain leaders of the Congress, there was an ambiguity, if we can call it that, between their democratic ideas and their profound Hinduism. Their political nationalism was at times indistinguishable from their religious fervor, although they did not adopt the aberrant form of Hinduism of Savarkar and his followers. Nehru was the great exception. His attempt to modernize India, which was partially realized, corresponds exactly to what he truly was. He was not, like his predecessors and associates, a soul divided by two traditions; his were rather a mind and sensibility torn apart by the nearly always tragic enigma of history. His waverings were due to the complexities of the circumstances, not to the influence of irreconcilable values and ideas. He loved India with a lucid love and, without sharing them, understood and accepted its contradictions. His love for Western civilization, on his rationalist and socialist side, was not stained by religious superstition, and he was able to see the Europeans as his equals. His anti-Western policies were the product of his years as a student at Harrow and Cambridge: there he learned to hate not only the English but imperialism itself.

Like many of his generation—some of the best among them—he did not understand, or refused to understand, the true moral and political significance of totalitarian Communism. It was a grave mistake, and he paid for it at the end of his days. But one must also say that Nehru, in the century of Hitler, Mao, and Stalin, was a civilized politician. A contradictory figure, like the age itself: an aristocrat who was a socialist; a democrat who exercised a kind of peaceful dictatorship; an agnostic governing a nation of believers; a man of moral ideals who did not, at times, disdain alliances and commitments that were less than impeccable. But all his errors are more than balanced by the positive aspects of his work. He was the heir of Gandhi, not his disciple or continuation. In fact, he moved India in a direction opposite to the one preached by the Mahatma: modernity. Nehru was the founder of the Republic, and his legacy may be summarized in three words: nationalism, secularism, and democracy.

Like Nehru's formative years at Cambridge, modern India cannot be explained without the influence of British culture, particularly the concept of nationalism. As a sentiment and as a historical reality, nationalism is as old as humanity: there has never been a society that did not feel itself united by a land, a language, and customs. As an idea, however, it is an invention of the modern Europeans, and it is an ideology as much as a sentiment. Like all sentiments, it may be altruistic or destructive—or grotesque. In countries like India or Mexico, which have been colonies and have suffered psychic wounds, nationalism is sometimes aggressive and deadly, and sometimes comic. I have heard Mexican journalists, and even one historian, claim that the reports of human sacrifice among the Aztecs and other Mesoamerican cultures were a hoax, a slander perpetrated by the Spanish to justify the Conquest. In India, a professor discovered that the lingam is an astronomical sign that the ignorant masses, deceived by the Europeans, had transformed into a phallic symbol.

Neither the Indians nor the Mexicans deny their past: they cover it over and repaint it. It is a process that is not entirely conscious, and that is its effectiveness, as a protection from criticism. It is a psychological vaccine. I once saw the erotic

temples of Konarak and Khajuraho described in a tourist bro-
chure as a kind of propaganda to stimulate matrimonial unions
at a time when the vogue for asceticism was threatening to
depopulate the country. In Tantrism, prolonged coitus without ejaculation is a ritual for reaching enlightenment; a modern interpretation explains it to us as a form of birth control.
When Nehru spoke in Parliament of the need to assimilate
modern science and technology, a member interrupted to re-
mind him that in the Vedic era the Indians had invented ways
of exploring outer space: "I cite a historical fact accepted by
science, in that the Purānas relate it." (Science now enjoys a
religious prestige; therefore it is natural to believe in religion
as a science.) Years ago, walking with a foreign friend who
had recently arrived in Mexico City, I showed him one of
our most beautiful avenues, the Paseo de la Reforma. He
looked at me in surprise and said, "But Mexico is a Catholic
country." I had to explain to him that the word "Reforma"
does not refer to the religious revolution of Luther and Calvin
that changed the world, but rather to some laws created by
President Benito Juárez in the last century. Similarly, in our
National School of Anthropology, the phrase "Western culture" does not refer to the civilization of Europe but to a
relatively primitive pre-Hispanic group in the northwest of
Mexico.

All this would be funny were it not frightening. Nationalism is not a jovial god: it is Moloch drunk with blood. In
general, the excesses of nationalism originate in the cult of
homogeneity that its believers profess: a single faith and a
single language for all. A popular advertising slogan perfectly
expresses this longing: "Just like Mexico, there's only one!"
But in India many nationalisms live together, and they are all
fighting with one another. One of them, Hindu nationalism,

wants to dominate the others and subject them to its law—like an Aurangzeb in reverse. Another, in Kashmir, wants the state to unite with a hostile nation, Pakistan—thus ignoring the lesson of Bangladesh, which had more in common with Pakistan than Kashmir does. Others, like the Sikhs and the Tamils, are separatists. On their part, the Muslims try to exempt themselves from various national laws when they are in contradiction with the mandates of the Sharī'a. A Muslim woman who was divorced asked for the pension to which she was entitled under Indian law. The Indian court ruled in her favor, but Rajiv Gandhi, afraid of alienating the Muslim vote, overturned the ruling, violating a fundamental right of all modern democracies: equality before the law, regardless of sex, race, or religion.

How can India deal with all these tendencies that threaten to return it to the eighteenth century, its century of anarchy and incessant war? The answer is in secularism. It began in 1868 with Queen Victoria's proclamation guaranteeing freedom of religion. It was perfected by the leaders of the Congress, consecrated by the Constitution, and incarnated in the figure of Nehru. Its principles are few and clear: no state religion; separation of temporal and religious power; equality before the law; freedom of belief; respect for the minorities and for the rights of individuals. Secularism is not only an abstract juridical principle, it is a concrete policy, subject to the daily test of reality. In the case of India, this reality is diabolically confused. The Constitution grants the central government vast powers to deal with separatist tendencies, but the abuse of these powers can often become counterproductive. This was the case with Indira Gandhi. Secularism implies impartiality, but impartiality in itself can be mistaken for impotence. True secularism requires tact, combining tolerance with strength, and its exercise is dependent on two conditions. The first is the separation of powers, so that the judiciary may block the abuses of the executive branch or the often partisan decisions of the legislature. The judiciary is the keeper of the rule of law, without which there is no social order. The second condition is governmental prudence. For Aristotle this was the cardinal virtue of politics. In the Middle Ages the good king was called "prudent." Without prudence, which is cruelly absent in modern democracies, both among the leaders and among the masses, good government is impossible.

A policy that is both secular and realistic must—in varying measures and according to circumstances—keep in mind both Western modernity and traditional values. For this reason, I have mentioned the two conditions that an effective secularism requires: one, which is modern, the English democratic legacy, the separation of powers; the other, which is timeless and belongs to both European and Indian tradition, prudence. In traditional Hindu thinking, the figure of the king, the warrior, and the man of action is inseparable from that of the Brahman, who represents wisdom and, in its highest expression, passion. The prudent king is he who controls his passions. Jean-Alphonse Benard has correctly observed that "the political problem of India, now as before, is not the irreconcilable conflict between tradition and modernity, authority and democracy, but the excessive polarization of power at the top."[*] In effect, this is what occurred in the Indira Gandhi administration, and also, in different circumstances, under Nehru. But one must bear in mind the traditional tendency toward separation and fragmentation. This is the reality that had to be confronted equally by the Maurya and Gupta em-

---

[*] Jean-Alphonse Benard, *L'Indie, le pouvoir et la puissance*, Fayard, Paris, 1985.

pires, by the Mughals and the British. It is a history of two thousand years of struggle between separatism and centralism.

The conflict between a central authority and local powers can be resolved only by a fusion of modernity (democracy and separation of powers) with traditional centralism. Except for exceptional figures like Ashoka and Akbar, political reality in India traditionally has been that of despotic power. The originality of the Indian project for nationhood is precisely its attempt to avoid the danger of despotism with the only known remedy: democracy. Of course, democracy can also be tyrannical, and the dictatorship of the majority no less odious than that of a single person or group. Thus the necessity for a separation of powers, a system of checks and balances. But the best laws in the world become dead letters if the leader is a despot, one who controls others because he is incapable of controlling himself.

A brief look at the modern histories of India and Latin America will help us understand the differences between the political evolutions of both regions. When one thinks of the Spanish Empire in the Americas, one is amazed by the vastness of the territory and the number and variety of cultures under its domain. The immensity of the distances, the heterogeneity of the populations, and the slowness and difficulty of communication hindered neither the generally peaceful government nor the harmony among the various regions. At the beginning of the nineteenth century, the kingdoms and provinces of the empire rose against their domination by Madrid. Unlike what happened in India, the struggle turned into a full-scale war. Once independence was achieved, a new brotherhood with political ambitions—the military—appeared, determined to impose its ideas by force. The Wars of Independence were the seedbeds for the *caudillos,* the local military bosses. With them began the sickness that is endemic to our societies: militarism and its consequences—coups d'état, uprisings, civil wars. In freeing ourselves from Spanish domination, we did not open the doors to modernity but to the past. The caudillos returned; the terrible, triple legacy of the Arabs, the Spanish, and the American Indians: the sheik, the *mandamás,* the cacique. In contrast, India achieved independence not by armed struggle but through a long democratic process. Thus it avoided the rise of the caudillos, those messiahs with epaulets and those revolutionary caesars who have proliferated in so many countries in Asia, Africa, and Latin America.

I have noted that one of the characteristics of the history of India has been the absence of a universal state that would unite all the various peoples of different languages and cultures. The British Empire, like the Spanish in America, was the agent of unification. But there the similarity ends. The British legacy was neither religious nor artistic, it was judicial and political; secularism occupies a central place in it. For example, the transition to Independence in India would have been impossible without the help of two secular institutions created by the British but composed of Indians: the army and the civil service. In Latin America, the army has been the principal catalyst of civil disorder; in India, it is the defender of order and the Constitution. As for the bureaucracy: we Latin Americans still have not been able to create a civil service comparable to those of Europe or Japan.

There is an intimate correspondence between secularism and democracy. A non-secular democratic state is not truly democratic; a non-democratic secular state is a tyranny. In India, secularism and democracy are the two complementary aspects of the legacy of Nehru. Both have suffered serious damage since his death, but they have resisted the double onslaught of political corruption and of nationalisms and regionalisms. I have frequently heard it said that in a country like India, with its immense demographic and social problems, what is essential is not democracy but attending to the economy and the needs of the people. No one can deny—certainly not a Mexican: our country suffers similar evils—that poverty in India reaches levels that are simultaneously pitiful and infuriating. But this argument ignores the immense progress that has been made in many areas, such as agriculture and certain branches of industry. Although the criticism of democracy has abated since the collapse of the "socialist" totalitarian nations, it is still worth confronting. In the first place, democracy is not an obstacle to modernization and economic and social development; on the contrary, it is often one of its conditions. In the places where the government has employed coercive methods to foster the economy, the initial, advantageous gains have led to disastrous results. Moreover, when deprived of basic rights—such as those of free association and the freedom to hold strikes—the workers end up with a minimal portion of the national product. Of course, democracy is not a panacea that cures all ills and automatically guarantees social justice. Nor is it a method for accelerating economic progress. But it is a way to ensure that progress is not realized at the expense of the majority. It is not a spur to production but rather an instrument for introducing a little justice into our terrible world.

One of the causes—perhaps the major cause—of the social and economic underdevelopment in India, as well as in Mexico, is the population explosion. In the case of Mexico, I have dealt with this subject in various writings, and will not repeat myself here. My reflections here do not deal with a subject that has already been abundantly discussed by many authorities, but rather with the paradox of an Indian state—modern, secular, and democratic—faced with societies that are to a large extent still traditional. In these pages I have been concerned with the political and ideological aspects of this question, but I must also mention, although only in passing, another determining factor. Apart from the existence of a central administration, a common law, and a political democracy that rules the entire country, there is a national network of economic and commercial interests, activities, and exchanges. This network is as strong as the political one. In the struggle against separatism, especially that of the Hindu nationalists, the national economic interests are the allies of the secularism of the state, as is the pluralistic cultural legacy, which contains the Buddhist Ashoka as well as the Muslim Akbar, Tagore the poet and Gandhi with his white cotton shirt stained with blood.

We are witnessing now, at the end of the century, the resurrection of ethnic and psychic passions, beliefs, ideas, and realities that seemed to have been long buried. The return of religious passion and nationalist fervor hides an ambiguous meaning: Is it the return of ghosts and demons that reason had exorcised, or is it the revelation of profound truths and realities that had been ignored by our proud intellectual constructs? It is not easy to answer this question. What can be said is that the revival of nationalism and fundamentalism—why don't they call it by its true name, fanaticism?—has become a great threat to international peace and the integrity of nations. In India, this threat is permanent and daily. I have said that the solution is double: secularism and democracy. The task is particularly difficult because it requires a delicate balance between federalism and centralism. Luckily, although

Hindu fanaticism is strong in the north, in Maharashtra and certain other regions, it is weak in the south. I believe that heterogeneity will work in favor of secularism and against the hegemonic pretensions of Hinduism.

Of course, it is impossible to foresee the future turn of events. In politics and history, perhaps in everything, that unknown power the ancients called Fate is always at work. Without forgetting this, I must add that, in politics as well as in private life, the surest method for resolving conflicts, however slowly, is dialogue. Talking with our adversary, we become our own interlocutor. This is the essence of democracy. Its preservation entails the conservation of the project of the founders of modern India: a state that encompasses diversity without suppressing it. It is a task that demands realism and imagination, and, at the same time, a certain virtue. There is a terrible law: all great historical creation has been built upon sacrifice. In the case of Indian democracy, the blood of a just man, Mahatma Gandhi, and also that of Indira, her son Rajiv, and countless innocent victims. All of them died so that one day Hindus, Muslims, Sikhs, and the others could talk in peace.

THE APSARĀ AND THE YAKSHI

In Hindu mythology, *apsarās* and *yakshis* are female creatures like our dryads and hamadryads. Apsarās—"moving in the water"—are the "daughters of pleasure," according to the *Rāmāyana,* and part of the "common treasure of the gods." Yakshis, more terrestrial and associated with the worship of trees, are lascivious; they frequently figure in Buddhist sculpture.

Although I have written more than I originally intended, I have touched on only a few historical and political matters. These are questions that concern us all, and couldn't be avoided. But I would have preferred to write about what I love and feel: India did not enter me through my mind but through my senses. I have spoken of my arrival in Bombay, one morning forty years ago: I can still breathe that humid air, see and hear the crowds in the streets, remember the brilliant colors of the saris, the murmur of voices, my dazzlement before the Trimurti in Elephanta. I have also mentioned in passing the food; from it I gained, early on, a small insight that taught me more about India than a monograph: I realized

137

that its secret is not a mixture of flavors, but rather a gradu-
ation of opposites that are simultaneously pronounced and
subtle. Not a succession, as in the West, but a conjunction. It
is a logic that rules nearly all Indian creations.

Music was another initiation, more extensive and more
noble; I confess that in that art, as in so many other things, I
continue to be a novice. I say this with a certain sadness,
considering that it has been my constant companion for years.
I listened to it in concert on memorable nights in the gardens
of Delhi, mingled with the rustle of the wind in the leaves;
other times I heard it slipping into my room like a sinuous
river, sometimes dark and sometimes sparkling. *Rāgas* are so-
liloquies and meditations, passionate melodies that draw circles
and triangles in a mental space, a geometry of sounds that can
turn a room into a fountain, a spring, a pool. What I learned
from music—besides the pleasure of walking through those
galleries of echoes and gardens of transparent trees, where
sounds think and thoughts dance—was something that I also
found in Indian poetry and thought: the tension between
wholeness and emptiness, the continual coming and going
between the two.

Sculpture was my first revelation and remains the most en-
during. Not only the works from the high periods, such as
those on Elephanta, but also the small wonders that are the
popular works, made of clay, metal, or wood, sonorous as
birds, fantastic forms born from the hands of anonymous
craftsmen. Indian sculpture is naturalistic, like that of Greece
or Rome, and is the aesthetic opposite of the sculpture of
ancient Mexico, that lover of terrible abstractions. But in their
folk arts the Indian and Mexican sensibilities converge: fantasy, humor, bright colors, bizarre shapes. The world of an
ordinary sacredness and of a daily poetry. The love of objects

that function as talismans, utensils, or toys is central to the Indian sensibility. Essential, too, is an affinity for nomenclatures, numbers, categories, and lists, whether of shapes, tastes or sensations, philosophical ideas or grammatical figures. Logic, grammar, aesthetics, and erotics are alike in this predilection for catalogs and classifications. The treatises on the erotic are dictionaries of positions, caresses, and sensations.

At the same time, there is a passion for unity. It is not by chance that India discovered the zero; nor that it was seen simultaneously as a mathematical concept and a metaphysical reality.* For Shankara, one is the limit of the thinkable; for Nāgārjuna, emptiness is. Between the one and the zero—incessant combat and instantaneous embrace—the history of Indian thought unfolds. The great questions about the reality of the world—What is it? How is it?—also encompass the question of origin: What was there at the beginning? Was there a beginning? In one of the most beautiful hymns of the *Rig Veda,* sometimes called the "Hymn of Creation," the poet tries to imagine how it was at the beginning and asks:

Then even nothingness was not, nor existence.
    There was no air then, nor the heavens beyond it.
What covered it? Where was it? In whose keeping?
    Was there then cosmic water, in depths unfathomed?

Then there was neither death nor immortality,
    nor was there then the torch of night and day.
The One breathed windlessly and self-sustaining.
    There was that One then, and there was no other.†

---

* Pre-Columbian Mexico also discovered the zero, but with different consequences: it figured only in numeration, not in religious philosophy.
† Translation by A. L. Basham, *The Wonder That Was India,* Macmillan, New York, 1954.

In the stanza that follows, desire descends, is implanted like a seed in the One, awakes, and the world is born. But the question of the first two stanzas—What happened *before?*—is not answered. (Nor does modern physics know the answer.) An initial and disturbing confession of ignorance: this primordial state is a *before* before the others. Nevertheless, anticipating Plotinus, the hymn implies that the One was before being and nonbeing, before duality. And the poet comments: "The sages who have searched their hearts with wisdom / know that which is, is kin to that which is not." All that can be said about being and nonbeing are in those enigmatic and sublime lines.

Idealist monism erects its grand constructions of thought through negations and erasures. The Absolute, the principle in whose matrix all contradictions dissolve (Brahma), is "neither this nor this nor this." No predicate confirms it, all are merely limitations. It is the way in which the great temples at Ellora, Ajanta, Karli, and other sites were built, carved out of mountains. A double and grandiose design: to sculpt mountains, to construct edifices of reasoning, based on a reflection of the abyss. There is an absolute correspondence of Hindu thought, its architecture, and its sculpture.

Buddhism has been no less bold. Its dialectics are a dizzying succession of ideas, one after the other destroyed by the knife of a logic that always quickly confronts us with the zero: *shūnyatā,* the indescribable unreal reality of emptiness. All these speculations have an equivalent—more exactly, a corporeal translation—in sculpture and painting. I have never seen presences more richly terrestrial than the figures of the donors (*dampati*) on the facade of the Buddhist sanctuary at Karli. They are earth and water, the most ancient things and the newest, changed into the bodies of men and women. Terrestrial and celestial elements not in moments of anger or joy—both of which are dangerous for mortals—but in an instant of peaceful sensuality. An instant as long as a century. Seeing these naked couples, sensual without cruelty, I understood the meaning of the word "benevolence." Those giant smiles are the incarnations of the syllable *Yes,* an enormous and carnal acceptance of life. A *Yes* as huge as the waves and the mountains. And yet, a great paradox, these sculptures guard a temple to emptiness, an altar to zero, a sanctuary of the *No.*

In Vidyākara's classic anthology of Sanskrit poetry,* the great majority of the poems are erotic. It is not strange that the compiler of these texts was a Buddhist monk. In Buddhist sanctuaries, as well as in those of the Jains and Hindus, erotic figures abound. Some temples, such as those in Khajuraho and Konarak, may be seen as manuals of sexual positions, sculpted *Kāma Sūtras.* The union of religion and eroticism, though less explicit and intense than in India, is also a feature of Hispanic literature in the sixteenth and seventeenth centuries: the most fervid and severe faith is combined with an exalted sensuality. In the ardent eroticism of the poetry of St. John of the Cross or the prose of St. Teresa, it is often difficult to distinguish between spiritual experience and physical sensation. Lope de Vega and Góngora, among others, were priests, and Juana Inés de la Cruz was a nun. In Vidyākara's anthology there are various poems attributed to a Dharmakīrti. Reading this name, I rubbed my eyes: was it possible that the author of these erotic poems was also the severe Buddhist logician? Professor Ingalls dispelled my doubts: the passionate, sensuous,

---

* *The Subhāsitaratnakosa, compiled by Vidyākara,* edited by D. D. Kosambi and V. V. Go-khala, Harvard Oriental Series, vol. 42, Cambridge, MA, 1957. In English: *An Anthology of Sanskrit Court Poetry,* translated by Daniel H. H. Ingalls, Harvard Oriental Series, vol. 44, Cambridge, MA, 1965.

and ironic poet and the closely reasoning and sharp-minded philosopher are almost certainly one and the same.

I cite the case of Dharmakīrti because he seems to me one example, among many, of this disconcerting union of thinking and sensuality, abstraction and delight in the senses. The philosopher Dharmakīrti reduces all rationalizations to absurdity; the poet Dharmakīrti, facing the body of a woman, does the same to his own dialectic. Dharmakīrti lived at the end of the seventh century. He was born in Trimalaya, in the south of India, and probably studied at the famous monastery of Nalanda. He left seven treatises on logic, various commentaries on the *sūtras,* and a handful of erotic poems. Dharmakīrti denied the authority of the Buddhist scriptures (but not the words of the Buddha) and argued that we indeed perceive reality, but our perception is momentary and ineffable; with the rest of its perceptions the mind constructs phantasmagoric entities that we call past and future, you and I. In one of his poems, he uses the example of a young woman's body to prove the truth of Buddhist doctrine:

PROOF
Her skin, saffron toasted in the sun,
eyes darting like a gazelle.

—That god who made her, how could he
have let her go? Was he blind?

—This wonder is not the result of blindness:
she is a woman, and a sinuous vine.

The Buddha's doctrine thus is proved:
nothing in this world was created.

This poem by Dharmakīrti could have been included in the Palatine Anthology; it has the economy and perfection of an epigram by Meleagros or Philodemus. It is simultaneously sensual, intellectual, and ironic: it exchanges a wink of intelligence with the reader. Although only a few poems of Dharmakīrti's survive, it is not difficult to discern in them a temperament that is both passionate and epigrammatic, in which there is a dialogue between the senses and the intelligence, a love for life and a disenchantment, as in this lapidary couplet:

> See this white-haired pillar of victory.
> I've won. Your arrows, Love, can't touch me.

Two lines by an anonymous poet display the same laconic perfection, created from precision and elegance:

> Admire the art of the archer:
> he never touches the body and breaks the heart.

The metaphor is as old as erotic poetry itself: glances are arrows that, although invisible, pierce bodies and souls. Dante and Cavalcanti used and abused the trope, as did Anacreon, Meleagros, and Ovid. The universality of the metaphor corroborates the universality of the sentiment.

Many of the surviving classical Sanskrit poems have a strange but undeniable similarity to Alexandrine poetry and its Roman successors, like Catullus. And also to Hellenistic sculpture: curves and muscles, full hips and firm breasts, broad masculine shoulders, women's thighs and arms fit for wrapping around another body: vines and tendrils twining around a column or a virile torso. Bodies made for the lively exercises of love, a poetry that is quite modern in its uninhibited praise of physical pleasure.

The other side of the coin: it is a mannered poetry, and one that is finally wearying like a month of banquets. What it lacks, I would dare to say, is silence and reticence. The greatest Sanskrit poetry, like the Greek and Latin, has eloquence, nobility, a sensuality of forms, violent and sublime passions. In sum, the plenitude of a great art. But—also like Greek and Latin—it doesn't know how to remain silent. It never knew the secret of the Chinese and Japanese: insinuation, oblique allusion. Its great merit is its corporeal and spiritual beauty, both of which are understood as the harmony of the parts of the whole. This said, I confess that my reservations are useless: to read these poems is to experience clarity. Their language is complex but never confusing; their ideas are limited but bright and sharply delineated; their forms are harmonious and rich. It is a poetry that ignores that which is beyond the eyes and the reason, all those infinites and transfinites that surround us, and that have been discovered by modern man. Yet it reminds us that to see is to think, and in so doing it reconciles the two greatest human faculties, seeing and understanding.

Classical Sanskrit poetry is little known in the West, where the translators and scholars have tended to concentrate on India's great religious and philosophical texts, on the epic poems (the *Mahābhārata* and the *Rāmāyana*), and on the mother lode of stories and fables. The poetry has been treated with a certain indifference, exactly the opposite of what has occurred in the West with classical Chinese and Japanese. And yet this poetry, which was written between the fourth and twelfth centuries, is contemporary with the height of ancient Indian civilization, and the temples, sculptures, and paintings that

anomasia, plays of words and meanings. The figures of speech (*alamkāra*) are numerous and have been studied by the critics with great subtlety and in minuscule detail. In the treatises on poetry there is an aesthetic category that is difficult to define in a Western language: *rasa*. The word means "flavor." Ingalls wisely prefers to translate it as "mood." In Spanish, it would be closer to *gusto,* taste: "the sensibility for the appreciation of beautiful things, and the criteria for distinguishing them" (María Moliner, *Dictionary of Spanish Usage*). The French— particularly the prose writers of the eighteenth century, and certain poets of the nineteenth, such as Baudelaire—have written with great taste on the subject of taste.

A revealing coincidence: neither the poets of ancient India nor the French writers of the second half of the eighteenth century—I am thinking, above all, of the libertine novelists— used vulgar words, and they almost always avoided explicit mention of the genitals. The exceptions in France were Restif de la Bretonne and Sade; although Sade, along with his periods of shocking language (which was, however, almost never colloquial), has others that are entirely historical or philosophical. One of the most celebrated eighteenth-century libertine novels is entitled precisely *Thérèse philosophe*. In Laclos, eroticism is mental, and the author portrays not what the characters are feeling, but what they are thinking while feeling or while watching the feelings of the victim-couple. In the small masterpiece by Vivant Denon, *Pas de lendemain,* the classical clarity of the language makes the erotic relation even more ambiguous. Something similar occurs in many classical Sanskrit poems. In neither case is the reticence of the authors due to morality. It is aesthetic, a question of taste: exactly the opposite of what occurred in modern literature.

Another quality that distinguishes Indian criticism: the idea of suggestion. One need not say it all: the poetry is in that which is not said. In this, the poets of classical India resemble the European symbolists or the Chinese or Japanese poets. But the resemblance to these last is superficial: the spirit of Sanskrit poetry, like that of Greek or Latin, is explicit and emphatic. The great charm of Chinese and Japanese poetry consists in its admirable reticence, something that is quite difficult to achieve in an Indo-European language. A third characteristic: impersonality. It is a trait shared by all the classical poetries, including the European, and also by Baroque poetry. For the classical poet, poetry is art, not confession. The author does not express his own sentiments but rather those of the personae of his poems: the lover, the abandoned woman, the hero. There is nothing less Romantic than kāvya poetry: the originality of the poet is not in the expression of his feelings and thoughts, but in the perfection and novelty of his tropes and images. There are exceptions, of course, such as Bhartrihari, where the voice of the poet filters through the sieve of the language. And in the ironical and sensual Dharmakīrti, the severe philosopher, there are sudden flashes of a personal intimacy that crack the conventions of the genre. Isolated infractions: the general rule is impersonality. It is worth clarifying that impersonality is not inauthenticity. True art simultaneously transcends mere artifice and subjective elaboration. Objective as nature itself, it introduces an element that does not appear in the natural processes, one that is entirely human: sympathy, compassion, irony.

Although much has been lost—due to the heat, the monsoons, insects, wars, invasions, and the lethargy of Hindu civilization since the thirteenth century—many poems have survived. There are collections of short poems, called "centuries," consisting of a hundred or more compositions on a single theme. These centuries are sometimes the work of a single poet; others, such as in the cases of Amaru and Bhartrihari, are merely attributions; many are written by a combination of authors. Amuru's century is largely erotic, and is highly esteemed. The three centuries of Bhartrihari—superbly translated into English by Barbara Stoler Miller—are equally famous, though not all the poems were written by the poet himself. The first century is devoted to a contemporary topic—the intellectual and the prince—but the poet tells us nothing original or new. The second, which is far superior, is on love; and the third, on religious life.

Lastly, the anthologies. The most famous is that of the Buddhist monk Vidyākara, a Bengali who lived at the end of the eleventh century. According to the scholar D. D. Kosambi, who discovered the anthology in an ancient library in Kathmandu, Vidyākara was an important dignitary in the Buddhist monastery of Jagaddala, which today is a heap of stones. We know nearly nothing about his life, but his anthology reveals a precise literary taste and an open and tolerant spirit. Although, as Ingalls points out, Vidyākara showed a preference for the poets of his own era (700–1050) and region, in his anthology there are not only poems dedicated to the Buddha and the Bodhisattvas but also to the Brahmanic gods: Shiva, Vishnu, Pārvatī, and others. Erotic poems, dealing with a love that is inseparable from the body and its encounter with other bodies, form the major part of the book. I should emphasize that what is most characteristic of Vidyākara's anthology—and of kāvya poetry in general—is the entirely profane nature of the majority of the poems. The veneration of the gods did not act as a censor. Nor is this a case of religious or mystical eroticism, as in the poems of St. John of the Cross or the Indian poems that sing of the love of Krishna for the cowgirl Rādhā. Moreover, eroticism is not the only topic: there are also poems on nature and its phenomena, the joys and pains of daily life, and death.

Vidyākara's *Treasury* is composed of 1,728 poems, fewer than those in the Palatine Anthology. The similarity between the two anthologies is extraordinary: brevity and concision, irony and sensuality, the multiplicity of themes and the attention to the characteristic detail, the presence of death and the humor or fear it provokes in us, familiarity and artifice, the endless repetitions and the sudden surprises. Each poem is an exquisite miniature, sharply drawn, amply modeled, a verbal cameo. A poetry that stays in the memory, that makes us both laugh and reflect.

The classical Sanskrit short poem, like the Greek or Latin, is an epigram. The word, despite what our dictionaries now say, does not refer merely to poems that are brief, satirical, or witty. The meaning is far wider: a composition that expresses in a few lines the drama of being human, its sensations, sentiments, and ideas. For that reason, these poems, though written more than a thousand years ago, are modern. Theirs is a modernity without dates. Civilizations are born, flourish, and disappear; one philosophy succeeds another; the railroad replaces the horse and carriage, and the airplane the railroad; the bow becomes a rifle which becomes a bomb . . . but people remain the same. Passions and sentiments hardly change. Although an Athenian from the fifth century B.C. or a Chinese from the ninth century would be amazed by telephones and televisions, he would understand perfectly the jealousy of Swann, Dmitri Karamazov's weakness to temptations, or the ecstasies of Constance and the gamekeeper Mellors. Human nature is universal, and it endures through all cultures and epochs. This is the secret of the perenniality of certain poems and books.

Although one of the major themes of Sanskrit poetry is physical pleasure, the attraction between men and women, the poems are often more ingenious than passionate. A quatrain by the poet Bhāvakadevī is a good example. The poet uses a political and military image to praise a woman's breasts:

> Her breasts are two brother kings, equal in nobility,
> looking out from the same heights, side by side,
> sovereigns of the vast provinces they have won
> in frontier battles, with a defiant hardness.

The union of the erotic and the martial—"fields of feathers for the battles of love," says Góngora—is as ancient as poetry itself. Apollinaire would have laughed at Bhāvakadevī's image, though he himself compared breasts to howitzer shells:

> Two flares
> Rose explosion
> Like two unbound breasts
> Insolently raising their nipples

The Hindu propensity for classifications, catalogs, and taxonomies also appears in Sanskrit poetry. Every part of the female body could be described by conventional images and expressions, and their tireless repetition forced the poets, who wrote for a small cognoscenti, to invent more and more complicated wordplays and witticisms. To take, almost at random, some examples of these metaphors and similes: the face of the female lover is the moon and its various changes; her breath, a spring breeze; her eyes, two fish; her neck, a tower, a column, a stalk; her eyebrows, two bows, two snakes; her way of walking may be like an elephant or a gentle wind in the leaves; her breasts, overflowing water jugs or two hills barely separated by a narrow path; her waist like a wasp, a young tree or a gazelle; her buttocks, two powerful spheres capable of sustaining the body of the universe; her pubis, a dark forested hill.... Many of these images also appear in Western poetry, although not with the same obsessive insistence. Others are barely mentioned by our poets. Speaking of the manner in which an adolescent is transformed into a woman, Ingalls writes: "The waist grows thin...and the three folds appear upon it [one of the signs of feminine beauty]. The loins and buttocks grow heavier, and the *romāvalī* appears." Ingalls explains: "The romāvalī is the vertical line of body-hair growing for a few inches above the navel. Being noticeable only on a woman of light complexion and very black hair, it was taken as a sign of beauty." It was also a sign of the sexual maturation of a woman:

> From the navel, barely a line,
> the romāvalī rises and glows,
> the pole of the banner love has
> planted in its new citadel.
>
> —LADAHACANDRA

A few pages later—but how many centuries do those few pages represent?—an anonymous poet responds:

> A firm stem, the romāvalī supports
> two lotuses opening: her compact breasts.
> House of two bees: her dark nipples.

These flowers tell of the treasure
hidden under her pubic mound.

The beauty of certain of the classical poems makes me think of Renaissance poets like Tasso: the triumph of a poetry of perfect features made of melodious lines, turning into sculpture and movement. The same love of ample forms, although the resemblance does not obscure profound spiritual differences. For example, a sentiment that is frequent in the poetry of Tasso and his contemporaries does not appear in Sanskrit poetry: melancholy. *La chair est triste* . . . In Indian poetry, on the other hand, there is a feeling that is rare in ours: luxuriousness, that moment in which the body, without losing its composure, seems to waver, enveloped by extreme pleasure, and falls into a delicious swoon. The poem becomes a naked body adorned with jewels, lying conquered. Luxuriousness is an effluvium that glows and vanishes. It is also an agent of metamorphosis: the male body, weakened by an excess of pleasure, twists into that of a woman; in turn, the female body, goaded by desire, leaps on top like a tiger. The transposition adds ambiguity to the erotic battle: Krishna seems at times like a maiden, and the graceful Pārvatī, in a flash of the eyes, turns into the terrifying Durga. In a famous collection of poems attributed to Bilhana (eleventh century?) one can read these lines:

Even now,
I remember my love's face:
golden earrings
grazing her cheeks
as she strove
to take the man's role,

beads of sweat strewn thick
like pearls
from the toil
of her rhythmic swinging.*

The inversion of positions in lovemaking is a constant theme. To avoid monotony, the poets resort to suggestion, saying it without saying it, as in this poem where the sounds and silences of jewelry hold a passionate dialogue:

When the ankle bracelet is still,
earrings and necklaces jangle;
when the man grows tired,
his determined lover relieves him.

The ambiguities of the erotic games that Kālidāsa, Amaru, and other poets describe are not perversions, in the Freudian sense: pregenital games. And, unlike the Greco-Roman classics, homosexuality hardly ever appears in the Indian poetic tradition. Nor is there the notion of sin or the consciousness of the transgression of norms. This is the great difference from Western eroticism, which since the end of the eighteenth century has been largely concerned with infraction and violence. Bataille emphasizes that eroticism is essentially transgression: Hindu erotic art proves him wrong. It is not a legal code but a fan: unfolding, refolding, unfolding again, displaying the whole range of pleasures. An art and a poetry that have never known sadism. (Scratches, however, have an emblematic function in the Indian erotic: the *Kāma Sūtra* enumerates the

---

* Translation by Barbara Stoler Miller, from *The Hermit and the Love-Thief*, Columbia University Press, New York, 1978.

various physical signs of sexual play—nail marks and tooth marks—and scrupulously codifies them.) To understand the difference between modern Western literature and that of Hindu India, one need only compare any text by Bataille with this poem by Kishitisa, so notable for its verbal and sensual refinement:

When will I see again her strong full thighs,
defensively closed, one against the other,
then opening, obedient to desire,
and as the silks slipped off, suddenly revealing,
like a wax seal on a secret treasure,
the marks, still moist, of my nails.

One of the tirelessly repeated motifs of the Palatine Anthology is that of the flickering lamp that illuminates the lovers' bedroom. The same motif appears in Sanskrit poetry. I particularly like this ingenious variation that combines the religious notion of *nirvāna*, which is extinction, with the quenching of the bright and blushing light:

The lamp of love had almost reached nirvāna
but it wanted to see what those two would do
when they were doing it: curious, it stretched its neck
and, seeing what it saw, let out a puff of smoke.

A poetry of visual images with a sense of humor, as in this combination of sensual intensity and confusion that one woman confides to another:

At the side of the bed
the knot came undone by itself,

and barely held by the sash
the robe slipped to my waist.
My friend, it's all I know: I was in his arms
and I can't remember who was who
or what we did or how.

—VIKATANITAMBĀ

In other poems, there is a delicate understanding of the contradictory impulses of adolescents, as in this remarkable quatrain by Kālidāsa:

Desire pushes her toward the encounter,
mistrust holds her back;
a silken banner, fluttering, limp,
furling and unfurling in the wind.

Another frequent motif is the description, in a few quick strokes, of the moment in which a young girl discovers that she is a woman. A girl bathing in a river or a lake is a universal theme. Here it takes on the intensity and clarity of a true apparition:

She shakes her hair
and in the chaos of her curls
bright drops shine.
She crosses her arms and studies
the growing freshness of her breasts.
A cloth clings, translucent, to her thighs.
Bending slightly, with a quick glance
toward the bank, she comes out of the water.

—BHOJYA-DEVA

Alongside the astonishment at the physical beauty of a young girl, the cunningness of this erotic invitation:

Traveler, hurry your steps, be on your way:
the woods are full of wild animals,
snakes, elephants, tigers, and boars,
the sun's going down and you're so young to be
   going alone.
I can't let you stay,
for I'm a young girl and no one's home.

To this oblique invitation, the poet Rudrata responds with one that is more open:

Here's where my aged mother sleeps,
and here my father, older than the oldest of the old,
here, like a rock, the slave girl sleeps,
and here I sleep, and I don't know for what sin
I deserve the absence, these days, of my husband . . .
said the young wife to the traveler.

Besides the games of passion and the sexual comedies, there are also the small events of ordinary life. These poems surprise us by their resemblance to certain situations in our own lives. One example is this peasant woman's half-burlesque and half-vindictive elegy on domestic labors:

When it comes to mending worn-out clothes
I have no rival in this world.
And I'm a master at the art
of making rich food with meager spices.
I am a wife.

                                —VĪRA

The fate of a schoolteacher is no less unfortunate than that of a poor man's wife. This poem could be the confession, between bitterness and disdain, of a professor today in some distant provincial university:

> I wear no bracelets
> golden as the autumn moon;
> I've never known the taste of the lips
> of a timid and tender young girl;
> I have never won, by sword or pen,
> fame in the halls of time:
> I wasted my life in broken-down colleges,
> teaching insolent, malicious boys.

A markedly physical and realistic, even materialistic, poetry—the irony of the blushing lamp whose flicker is inextricable from a sacred concept like nirvāna—becomes, at certain moments, a sober pessimism. A terrifying realism: true liberation, the ideal of Hindu civilization, is found only in death:

> He crossed the rivers of desire
> and now, immune to pain and joy,
> cleansed, in the end, of impure thoughts,
> reaches happiness with closed eyes.
> —Who and where?
>   —Can't you see him?
> That old flabby corpse in its shroud.

The feeling for nature is quite alive in Indian poetry. A fountain of marvels and wonders, the natural world can also be the occasion for a gnomic poetry:

It neither thunders nor hails,
shoots no lightning bolts,
nor unleashes great winds:
this huge cloud simply rains.

The natural world lives in continual struggle. In the jungles, mountains, and deserts swarm ferocious animals such as snakes and tigers, and supernatural creatures that are no less terrible: ogres, giants, monsters. Yet, there are also trees, the emblems of a quiet and kind strength:

Under the pitiless sun
it gives its shade to others,
and for others are its fruit.
A good man is like a tree.

Although the poets of ancient India knew neither publishing houses nor publicity nor best-sellers, they were not unaware of literary battles—or of irony:

Kālidāsa and the other poets?
Well, we're poets too.
The galaxy and the atom
both are matter: both exist.

—KRISHNABHATTA

Fame has always been equivocal, and poets have always simultaneously sought and disdained it:

"Who are you?"
                    "Fame."

"Where do you live?"

"I wander."

"And your friends,
Eloquence, Wealth, and Beauty?"
"Eloquence lives in Brahmā's mouth,
Wealth sleeps in Vishnu's arms,
Beauty shines in the globe of the moon.
Only I am left with no home in this world."

—CHITTAPA

A poem in praise of the poem that says without saying, the suggestion that both hides and reveals:

Beauty is not
in what the words say
but in that which they say without saying it:
not naked, but through a veil,
breasts become desirable.

—VALLANA

And the confidence in—the hope of—the appearance of a future reader, that twin soul who will save us from the injustices of the present, is a sentiment that runs through all poets and writers, both Eastern and Western:

Armed with their rules and precepts,
many condemn my verses.
I don't write for them,
but for that soul, twin to mine,
who will be born tomorrow.
Time is long and the world wide.

—BHAVABHŪTI

As one can see from these few examples, the poets of ancient India, despite the centuries and the differences in language, custom, and belief, are in many ways our contemporaries. A young poet at the end of the twentieth century could have written this poem by Dharmakīrti:

> No one behind, no one ahead.
> The path the ancients cleared has closed.
> And the other path, everyone's path,
> easy and wide, goes nowhere.
> I am alone and find my way.

Indian poetry is erotic, satirical, philosophical, and ultimately poetic, a criticism of poetry: a song and a meditation on song. Like all the poetic traditions of all languages, Sanskrit poetry has its weak points: formalism, a love for useless complications, repetitiveness, and a tendency toward softness. This last has always been seen in the West, whether morally or aesthetically, as a vice. The ancient rhetoricians warned the poets and orators against a style that was too elaborate and ornamental, which they called "Asiatic." The criticism seems just, at least if one thinks of certain texts such as the *Gītā-Govinda,* the famous poem by Jayadeva (thirteenth century). I have read it various times, in different French and English translations; the result invariably has been, after initial dazzlement, fatigue and boredom. It is not only the flaccidity but also the excessive aesthetic formalism: a love poem (the adulterous and sacred love of Krishna and Rādhā) ruled by an art of strict prescriptions. Passion turned into ballet. I realize that my severity is based not on the perfection of the poem, which is undeniable, but on the genre to which it belongs. It seems to me more remote than the pastoral novels of the sixteenth and seventeenth centuries. (Cervantes made fun of them, but he wrote one.) The *Gītā-Govinda* is a lyric and dramatic poem that tells an erotic and religious tale through a series of recitatives, each followed by a song of varying stanzas. The songs have different melodies (rāgas). A union of music and lyrical and dramatic poetry. It is not strange that the poem—and its numerous imitations—has in turn inspired a pictorial genre: the miniatures that illustrate the love of the god and the cowgirl.

The structure of the poem is extraordinarily complex, not only because of the relation between music and word, but also because of the variety of meters employed by Jayadeva, and his frequent use of alliteration, rhyme, and metaphor. According to the scholars, there is more than an echo of Kālidāsa in Jayadeva. At the same time, a folk element appears in the *Gītā-Govinda*, one new to classical poetry, which previously had been written only for a minority; this accounts for the poem's extraordinary popularity and countless imitations. In its formal perfection, the genre recalls the Italian madrigal and the poems of Tasso set to music by Monteverdi. But the madrigal is short and strictly lyrical, whereas Jayadeva's long poem is more related to theater and narrative. It is a kind of lyric drama. In the interesting study that accompanies her excellent translation of the text, Barbara Stoler Miller says that the songs, with their complex rhythmical structures, "create a sensuous surface of verbal ornamentation that suggests comparison with the sculptured surfaces of the temples of Bhubaneshwar or Khajuraho."* The observation is correct: Sanskrit poetry, which is both emotional and palpable, evokes

---

* *Love Song of the Dark Lord: Jayadeva's Gitagovinda*, edited and translated by Barbara Stoler Miller, Columbia University Press, New York, 1977.

the plasticity of sculpture. Like bodies, like the forms on sculptures and reliefs, the words see and touch.

Jayadeva's is the last great poem in the Sanskrit tradition. At the same time, it is the beginning of another tradition in the vernacular languages. At the end of the fourteenth century, in the north of India and in Bengal, there arose various poets who also sang the love of the god for the cowgirl, uniting religious devotion with a no less intense sensuality, and accompanied by music and paintings or prints. Among these poets, all of them more spontaneous and direct than Jayadeva, there are some of great merit, such as Vidyāpati, Chandī Dās, the poet-princess Mīrā Bāī, and Sur Dās. One can admire Jayadeva, but these poets accomplish what he could not: they enchant and move us. The successors of Jayadeva, according to W. G. Archer, did not follow him blindly. Their subject was not only the separation of Krishna and Rādhā but the whole history of their love. Moreover, they "roved freely over the many phases of their lovemaking, subjecting every incident to delighted analysis."*

It is not difficult to understand the delight the poets took in analyzing these episodes, nor that of the audience upon hearing them: in this love there is a passionate and subversive element. Rādhā is married and of humble birth (she guards the cattle of her village); Krishna is a prince and a god. A subversion of the social order, and a leaping of the distance that separates human beings from gods. Many of the episodes provoke laughter from the audience, as when Krishna, trying to slip into Rādhā's house, disguises himself as a flower seller or a doctor. Others are more ambiguous: there is a scene

---

* W. G. Archer, *The Loves of Krishna in Indian Painting and Poetry*, Grove Press, New York, 1958.

where Krishna is dressed in Rādhā's clothes, and she in the clothes of her divine lover. In another episode, Krishna surprises Rādhā bathing in the river. An unforgettable vision of the waking of desire: that moment when Rādhā discovers with panic and joy that, under the cloth of her shirt, her nipples are erect. A double surprise: Krishna surprising the bathing Rādhā, who is surprised discovering her own body.

CHASTITY AND LONGEVITY

Hindu eroticism is quite ancient and, as one may see in the *Kāma Sūtra* and other texts, has characteristics that sharply distinguish it from the Chinese or Arabic, as well as from the European. I have devoted a small book to this subject, and there is no need to repeat it here.* The pole opposite to sexual license is chastity. With an unsurpassable concision, the poet Bhartrihari (seventh century?) writes:

Why all these words and empty prattle?
Two worlds alone are worth a man's devotion.
The youth of beautiful women wearied by heavy breasts
And full of fresh wine's heady ardor for sport,
Or the forest . . .†

The desire for sexual pleasure, or the hermit's desire for liberation from the chain of rebirths in his mountain cave or forest retreat. The difference between Hindu and Christian asceticism is even more marked than those between their erot-

---

* *Conjunctions and Disjunctions*, translated by Helen Lane, Viking Press, New York, 1974.
† Translation by Barbara Stoler Miller, from *Bhartrihari: Poems*, Columbia University Press, New York, 1967.

icism. The key word of Western eroticism—I am referring to the modern West, from the eighteenth century to the present—is violation, which is an affirmation of the moral and psychological order. For Hindus, the key word is pleasure. Similarly, in Christian asceticism, the central concept is redemption; in India, it is liberation. These two words encompass opposite ideas of this world and the next, of the body and the soul. Both point toward what has been called the "supreme good," but there the similarity ends: redemption and liberation are paths that lead from the same point—the wretched condition of man—in opposite directions. For us to begin to understand this divergence, it is worth defining the place that sexual abstinence has in the ethical and religious traditions of India and of the West. Both deal with the same practice, but their religious and philosophical bases, their meanings and goals, are quite different.

The origin of the Christian cult of chastity is not in the Bible but in Greek philosophy, particularly Platonism. Nature and the body are not condemned in Genesis or the other books of the Old Testament. The Bible condemns adultery, incest, onanism (coitus interruptus), homosexuality, and other forms of sexual congress that were considered aberrant or even blasphemous by Hebrew ethics. The latter forms were generally orgiastic, often deriving from fertility cults, and were considered by Jewish thought to be relapses into polytheism. They were seen as religious deviations, a return to the ancient idolatry. The Gospels themselves do not condemn sex or the body.

In the Greek philosophical tradition, however, adopted by the fathers of the Church and the medieval scholasticists, the condemnation of the body is explicit. It is a natural consequence of the conception of the human being as a conjunction of body and soul, one perishable and subject to corruption, the other immortal. The idea of a soul distinct from the body is not, contrary to perception, native to Greece; it comes from abroad and does not figure, for example, in Homer. It appears in some of the pre-Socratics, such as Pythagoras and Empedocles; later Plato revived, refined, and formulated it in a magisterial and definitive manner in certain unforgettable passages in the *Phaedo* and *Phaedrus*. Even in the *Symposium* the contemplation of the beautiful body is only a rung on the ladder toward the vision of the supreme good: form, archetype, idea. In the *Phaedo*, the soul, prisoner of its mortal body, recalls its previous life among the other immortal souls; in the *Laws*, the body is condemned. With less strictness than his master, Aristotle believed that the greatest happiness to which a wise man could aspire was the contemplation, detached from the corporeal passions, of the movement of the stars, the image of the order of the universe. Plotinus and his disciples carried Platonic rigor to its extreme.

Christianity is the religion of the incarnation of God in a man and of the resurrection of the body, a doctrine that was scandalous both to the Gnostics and the Neoplatonists. Christian faith, St. Augustine warns us, is not Manichean. Nevertheless, the theologians and the Church ultimately adopted the condemnation of the body. Even certain Christian philosophers, such as Origen, exaggerated the Platonic critique. It is not difficult to understand why the Church adopted—although not entirely, and with certain reservations—this negative vision of the body. From the beginning—that is, from St. Paul—the interlocutor of Christianity was not pagan polytheism but Greek philosophy, which had believed in a unifying principle and had elaborated a metaphysics and an ethics incomparably richer than that of Jewish monotheism. The Church fathers faced an enormous task: How explain, how even think of, a unique creator God, both a person and an impersonal principle, without recourse to the terms and concepts of Greek philosophy? Or, to put it another way: How apply to the Christian God the teachings and attributes of the Unmoved Mover of Aristotle or the Unity of Plotinus? They had to create a bridge between the Being of philosophy and the God of the Gospels. It was a task that took centuries, reaching its fulfillment only with St. Thomas Aquinas. The same occurred with the ethics of the Stoics and with the necessary distinction between the immortal soul and the mortal body. Without that distinction it would not have been possible to find a philosophical basis for the Christian concept of the human person or of Christ's redemption. Whom does Christ redeem? Man, a creature whose immortal soul has been stained by Original Sin. But man is a composite of soul and body. Here the victory of Platonism is only partial. The doctrine of the resurrection of the body does not condemn the flesh: it transforms it and literally saves it, giving it immortality.

Christianity probably would not have adopted Plato's pessimistic vision had it not been for two ideas that, although they do not appear in Greco-Roman tradition, are the true sources of the Christian attitude toward the body: the belief in a unique God, creator of the universe, and the notion of Original Sin. These two ideas are the spinal column of Judaism and Christianity, and the point of convergence of the two. In the story in Genesis, God makes man from the primordial mud, and his companion from one of his ribs. A material creation, like that of a sculptor with wood or stone. Adam is made of mud, and Eve is "bone of [his] bones and flesh of [his] flesh." The first divine mandate is to be fruitful and multiply. Far from condemning the body, Yahweh exalts its genetic powers. Adam and Eve are not like the souls described by Plato in the *Timaeus*, who descend from the empyrean, cross the heavens, receive the fortunate and unfortunate influences of the planets, and become incarnate in a body subject to sickness, accidents, passions, and death. Adam and Eve are earth made flesh, animated by divine breath. Their sin was not sexual union—that was their cosmic duty: to multiply—but rather disobedience.

In Eden there are two trees, the tree of life and the tree of the knowledge of good and evil. The fruit of the first is the food of immortality, and while Adam and Eve live in the Lord's garden they will not know death. As for the other tree, God expressly forbids them to eat its fruit. A strange prohibition, for it is the fruit of supreme knowledge, and he who eats it will be like God. That, at least, is what the serpent tells Eve. There are many interpretations of this controversial passage (Genesis 3): Was the serpent lying to Eve? If it was lying, why did God call the fatal tree "the knowledge of good and evil"? In the end, whatever our interpretations may be, Adam and Eve ate the fruit and God expelled them from Eden. Their failure was disobedience. But the root of that failure is something infinitely more serious: they preferred themselves. Their sin was not loving God, their creator, but instead loving themselves and wanting to be gods. Men are as free as the angels and, like them, make bad use of their freedom: they want to divinize themselves. They imitate Satan and his hosts. Within this conception is a condemnation of the love of the body. But Christianity does not condemn the body as much as the excessive love of the body. To love a body exclusively is one of the ways in which man loves himself and forgets

God and his fellow men. The Platonic condemnation of the body was made to reinforce the notion of Original Sin: the shameful preference of the creature for itself. The true idol of mankind is man himself.

From the Hindu perspective, the story in Genesis is meaningless. Apart from certain incoherencies in the narrative, there is an idea that is difficult for Hindu tradition to accept: the notion of a creator God. The question of the origin of the world and of humanity appears in the *Rig Veda*, but the answer, as we have seen, is another question. In general, the Hindu sacred books say that the universe is the result of the working of mysterious and impersonal laws. Some of the texts state that time (*kāla*) or desire (*kāma*)—a sort of cosmic will, like that in Schopenhauer—"is the force that moves the changes of the universe." A stanza of the *Atharva Veda* (19.53) says, "Time [kāla] created the Lord of Creatures, Prajapāti," the creator demiurge.* From the Vedic era on, religious thought knew a unifying principle, which the Upanishads called *brahman*, the being of the cosmos, and which is identical to *ātman*, the being of man. Yet they never inferred from this principle the existence of a god who was the creator of the world and of men. That which is divine, not a divinity, is the creative force and the matrix of the universe. The idea of Original Sin, the consequence of the first disobedience, in which the shameful love of man for himself and his indifference to the Other and to the others, is incomprehensible to Indian tradition. The universe was not created, and thus there is no Lord, no command, no disobedience.

The Indian divinities, like those of Greece and Rome, are

---

* See Franklin Edgerton, *The Beginnings of Indian Philosophy*, Harvard University Press, Cambridge, MA, 1965 (a collection of texts from the *Rig Veda*, the *Atharva Veda*, the Upanishads, and the *Mahābhārata*).

sexual. Among their powers is an immense procreative force that makes them endlessly couple with all kinds of living things and produce new individuals and species. The activity of the universe is sometimes seen as an enormous divine copulation. The mythological stories are tales of the couplings and battles of the gods, goddesses, and their heroic progeny. The God of the Bible is a neuter god, the opposite of Zeus and Vishnu, Venus and Aditī, who are always in search of another lover. In a tradition of gods and goddesses in a perpetual state of heat, it is impossible to condemn sexual love, unless, as it happened in Greece, philosophy first makes a critique of mythology and of the gods themselves. But India had no Xenophanes. To the contrary, Indian philosophy always depended on religion; it was an exegesis, not a criticism. And when it broke with religion, it was in order to found a new religion: Buddhism. Among the creative forces of the universe, the texts often emphasize sexual desire. One reads in the *Atharva Veda:* "Desire [Kāma] was the first to be born; neither gods nor [departed] ancestors nor men have reached [equalled] him: [he is] superior to all and the most powerful." (9.2). And in another hymn: "Desire arose in the beginning, which was the first seed of thought." (19.52). To condemn the body and human sexuality in a tradition like Hinduism would be to condemn the gods and goddesses, the manifestations of a powerful cosmic sexuality. Hindu chastity and asceticism must have another source.

Sexual pleasure is, in itself, valuable. For Hindus, it is one of the four goals of man. Besides being a cosmic force, one of the agents of the movement of the universe, desire (kāma) is also a god, similar to the Greek Eros. Kāma is a god because desire, in its purest and most active form, is sacred energy: it moves humanity and all of nature. Within this vision of sexuality as cosmic energy and of the body as a reserve of creative energy is one of the reasons, probably the most ancient reason, for sexual abstinence. The body, like nature itself, is life that produces life: the seed in the earth, the semen in a womb. The human body not only stores life, it transforms its energy into thought, and thought into power. Chastity began by being a practice directed toward storing life and vital energy. It was a recipe for longevity and, according to some, immortality. This idea is fundamental to yoga and Tantrism, and it is central to Taoism.* Life is energy, physical and psychic power; sex is power and a fertilizing power that multiplies itself; the body is a source of sexuality and thus of energy. To retain semen (*bidu*), to guard it and transform it into psychic energy, is to appropriate the great natural and supernatural powers (*siddhi*). The same occurs with feminine sexual discharge (*rajas*). A Tantric text says: "The bidu is Shiva and the rajas is Shakti [his lover]; semen is the moon and rajas the sun." Therefore, although pleasure is one of the goals of man, the wise man casts it aside and seeks the path of abstinence and solitary meditation. Pleasure is desirable but finite; it does not save us from death or free us from future incarnations. Chastity gives strength for the great battle: breaking the chain of rebirths.

THE CRITIQUE OF LIBERATION

According to traditional ethics, human life has four goals: *artha, kāma, dharma*, and *moksha* (or *mukti*). Artha refers to the world of success and material gain. Kāma, the domain of

---

* See *Conjunctions and Disjunctions.*

pleasure and sexual life, is ruled not by self-interest but by desire. Dharma encompasses the higher life: the duties, morals, and principles that regulate the conduct of the individual toward family, caste, and society. Moksha is the liberation from the chains of existence, a breaking of the cycle of infinite transmigrations and its monotonous refrain:

> Birth, and copulation, and death.
> That's all, that's all, that's all, that's all,
> Birth, and copulation, and death.*

The four goals are all legitimate, but on the scale of values pleasure is superior to business, duty to pleasure, and liberation to the other three. He who seeks liberation does not see his body as an obstacle, but rather as an instrument. Ascetic practices, even the most severe, are a progressive mastering of the body. The yogi does not seek to separate his soul from his body, like the Platonic mystic; he wants to convert it into a weapon of liberation. Or, more exactly: into a trampoline that will spring him into the Absolute. Asceticism, in all its manifestations, coincides at one extreme with the erotic and at the other with the athletic. Moksha is the heroic answer to the miserable condition of man and the causes of that condition. Hindus and Buddhists share the Christian belief in our essential misery, but their explanation for its causes is quite different. It can be summarized by two terms: *samsāra* (the cycles of existence) and karma. These two words occupy the same place in Indian religious thought as the creation of man and Original Sin in Christianity. The Christian triad:

---

* T. S. Eliot, "Sweeney Agonistes."

Creation, Original Sin, Redemption. The Indian triad: Samsāra, Karma, Moksha.

The moral life is ruled by each individual's dharma, according to his caste and personal characteristics. It is not easy to define the word: it is "virtue" in the Greco-Roman or the modern sense, but it also signifies moral rules, correct conduct, and divine law. For Buddhists, dharma is the doctrine itself and therefore includes a vast amount of material: not only the various forms of Buddhism (such as Hīnayāna, Mahāyāna, and Tantra) but also the canonical texts in various languages (Pali, Sanskrit, Chinese, Tibetan, and so on). Yet the term is not imprecise, because there is a nucleus of beliefs, common to all the sects, that is the essence of Buddhism.* Thus dharma is doctrine, an ideal of life, an ethical code, a rectitude of deed and thought. In its highest and most pure expression, as Krishna explains to Arjuna in the *Bhagavad-Gītā*, it is the act that we perform without seeking any gain, because it is our duty. In a certain sense, it a version of the Kantian "categorical imperative." But the fulfillment of dharma does not bring us true happiness, which can only be found in the liberation from the ties that bind us to an existence that flows into death and an inevitable rebirth and a new dying. Dharma does not stop the wheel of transmigrations.

The belief in transmigration is one of the basic tenets of Indian religious thought and is shared by Hinduism, Buddhism, and Jainism. It is not a strictly rational concept; it is an article of faith. Nevertheless, it is considered to be a fact that no one can doubt. Samsāra encompasses all living things, from larvae to the gods. What turns the wheel of

---

* For many of the Buddhist schools, especially the Madhyamika, dharma is in itself the essential component of reality.

transmigrations? One of the Buddhist scriptures says: "The being is bound to samsāra, karma is his [means for] going beyond."* That is, karma takes the individual to his rebirth. Karma means "act," but it also, and above all, implies the consequences of our acts. We are the children, not of our parents, but of what we were in past lives. Hindus speak of "karmic law," and Buddhists of the "chain of causality." The idea is clear: each act, like everything in this world, has a cause which necessarily occurred earlier in time. Thus karma is the effect of every action, whether in this life, in the past, or in the future. This belief is also shared by the three religions. It is one of the four holy truths of Buddhism. In the sermon at Sarnath, the Buddha "began to turn the wheel of the law," that is, he articulated the doctrine and summarized it in Four Truths. The first is the truth of suffering and human misery (*duhkha*): "Birth is sorrow, age is sorrow, disease is sorrow, death is sorrow." The second truth: suffering "arises from craving, which leads to rebirth, which brings delight and passion and seeks pleasure . . . the craving for continued life, the craving for power." The third: "the stopping of sorrow" by "the complete stopping of that craving." The fourth truth is the way to stop the wheel of samsāra through the Eightfold Path that leads to liberation and nirvāna.

Liberation is not salvation in the Christian sense. There is no person or soul to be saved: the liberated is liberated from the illusion of the ego, his being becomes Being. Liberation is not a rebirth in the kingdom of the heavens, but rather a dismantling of the double fatality that ties us to this world and its meaningless turning: moksha liberates us from the burden

---

* Samyutta-nikāya I, 38. In *Buddhist Texts*, edited by E. Conze, I. B. Horner, D. Snellgrove, and A. Waley, London, 1954.

of karma that makes the wheel of samsāra turn. Liberation may be achieved in this world (*jīvan-mukti*, liberated in life) or in the other. The liberated ceases to exist in time and enters the Absolute. Thus, he knows immortality but does not know duration: moksha erases the differences of yesterday and today and tomorrow, between here and there. The liberated lives in an eternal present and inhabits a place that is all places and nowhere. For him it is always here and now. Everything begins with a free act: the renunciation of the world. From this negative decision a persistent, daily, positive action must follow. It is a paradoxical enterprise, because it is an activity destined to attain a state of nonactivity. In search of tranquillity, one must subject the body to a violation of physiological laws, and the spirit to the impossible: thinking without thoughts. A continual interpenetration between the mental and the corporeal, between feeling oneself touched by thought and thought by touch or sight, an unmoving movement of a solitary meditation that endlessly unweaves what it weaves, until it reaches a state of indescribable beatitude: *ānanda*.

Moksha is a gnosis and a praxis. First, it is a knowledge. Not in the modern sense of knowing—which has been generally reduced to information about this or that—but in the more ancient sense of *realizing* the truth: that is, making it real and effective, living it and becoming one with it. Moksha is self-knowledge. To understand oneself, one must practice introspection and eliminate the superfluous: karma and all that goes with it, enthusiasms, dislikes, nostalgia, affection, ego, personal consciousness. In that way one discovers that one's true self is other. This self has, according to the different schools and religions, various names: *ātman, sat, purusha*. It is also emptiness. It is neither an I nor a you nor a he nor a she.

It is neither a noun nor a pronoun. It has no weight, size, age, taste: it only is.... As a praxis, moksha is an asceticism, closely tied to yoga and its disciplines. Yoga permeates all the ancient Indian religions and philosophies. It is probable that it existed on the subcontinent before the arrival of the Aryan tribes and that it is an extraordinarily subtle and complex elaboration of prehistoric shamanic rituals and beliefs. Its practice is inseparable from the notion of power (*siddhi*) and it is saturated with the vices of magic. To repeat: archaicism and subtlety, gnosis and praxis, moksha is a paradoxical state that is both negative and positive. Negative because it is a liberation from the ties that bind us to the world and to time; positive because the Absolute is beatitude. Samkara says: "Moksha is eternal, but it experiences no changes ... it is omnipresent like the air, free of alteration, self-sufficient, and it is not composed of parts: it is one ... it is Brahman (the Self)."

Liberation is the work of hermits, and the joy of beatitude is solitary. The others never appear in any of the great Indian texts that deal with this subject. It is one of the great differences from Christianity and also, to a lesser extent, from Greek philosophy. The ancient Indians were interested in the art and science of politics, as is demonstrated by the thought of Kautilya, but they were concerned with power, how to acquire it and how to retain it. The idea of a just society forms no part of the Hindu philosophical tradition. It has been argued that the concept of dharma compensates for this omission, but I disagree: dharma is an ethic, not a politics. The difference from the Christian ideal is even greater and more radical: to save oneself, for a Christian, is to enter into the Kingdom of Heaven. A kingdom is a collective entity, and heaven is a perfect society of the blessed and the saintly. It is the opposite of the solitary liberated Hindu. Nor do the

Hindu texts—with one exception, which I will refer to later—extol civic action, unlike the Greeks, Romans, and Chinese. Confucius' thinking is essentially political. Plato and Aristotle wrote books on politics, and both saw civic action as one of the highest paths of virtue and wisdom. They did not, of course, believe that politics was the road to wisdom; they thought, more exactly, that the descent of wisdom into the city and its transformation into action were the essence of politics. In the case of Christianity, politics is permeated with religion and may be summarized by one word: charity. Christian thought, from the beginning, in its dialogue with the Roman Empire, and throughout the Middle Ages, conceived and developed political systems unknown to Hinduism and Buddhism. The difference from China is even more radical—and thus the indignation of many Chinese intellectuals at the spread of Buddhism in their country.

It is obvious that there is an opposition between the contemplative life of the mystic or the philosopher and the active life of the politician. Yet in our philosophical tradition—whether in antiquity, Christianity, or modernity—there has been a continual search for bridges between action and contemplation. The same occurred in China. That said, one must add that at the end of the *Enneads,* having spoken of the contemplation of the Unity, the Supreme, Plotinus says that "the blessed frees himself from the things here below and begins his solitary flight to the Solitary" (VI.11). The solitary, contemplating the Unity, discovers that it is he himself: he who contemplates sees himself in that which he contemplates. Here is the great difference between Christianity and the pagan philosophies. For the latter, in the dialogue between man and the Absolute, there is no place for other men. But is it really a dialogue? The Being of Greek philosophy is self-sufficient: it hears men but does not respond; it is contemplated by them but does not see them. Neither the Unity nor the eternal Forms nor the Unmoved Mover are figures of redemption. Antiquity knew no Savior or Redeemer. To know and to see the Being, for a Greek or Roman, was the supreme happiness, a sublime experience but one without communication. The same occurs (with one exception) in the Indian tradition: Brahman, Sat, and the other entities are loved without reciprocity. And the Buddha? He is not a god made flesh in order to save mankind; he is a man who renounced being a god in order to teach mankind the way toward solitary liberation.

The unilateral character of liberation naturally has a few exceptions, though not many. I have already spoken of Krishna. I will return to him in a moment, but first I would like to briefly mention the Bodhisattvas. Early Buddhism (Hīnayāna) venerated the figure of the *arhat,* a wise man or saint (in the tradition, it is the same thing) who reaches nirvāna, or enlightenment. He is free of the chain of karma: he is an Absolute. The arhat is a solitary contemplative. Mahāyāna Buddhism conceived of the Bodhisattvas, beings who had temporarily renounced the blessed state of Buddhas in order to help living creatures on their slow pilgrimage to enlightenment. The Bodhisattvas are neither gods nor, in the strict sense, humans, although they were humans in past lives. They are entities whose nature is emptiness. That is, they are nonentities. Their reality is paradoxical and indescribable. They are the liberated who have renounced nirvāna, but who, nevertheless, have the clairvoyance of those who have reached it. The Bodhisattvas bring together two virtues that the Buddhist scholar Edward Conze has rightly called contradictory: wisdom (*prājña*) and compassion (*karunā*). In the first place, they are Buddhas whose compassion has led them to defer the final awakening. They reached the state of Bodhisattva through the path of solitary wisdom, which, in turn, opens the doors to compassion. Wisdom is the origin of compassion, not the other way around. Buddhism does not exalt the "poor in spirit." To reach nirvāna, good works are not enough, one must also attain knowledge. What matters is the experience of truth, *being* in truth. Like Hindu liberation, Buddhist enlightenment is a solitary experience. Certainly the Bodhisattvas are figures of salvation; like our saints, they are disposed to help simple mortals. Yet, though their good deeds are innumerable, they are all of a spiritual nature. The Bodhisattvas do not know true and simple charity; they offer the bread and water of knowledge, not the real bread and water that alleviates hunger and thirst.

Moksha is a religious and philosophical ideal. It frees the heroic individual who seeks the arduous path of austerities, but it ignores one aspect of freedom. For us in the West, freedom has a political dimension. We are always asking ourselves what is the nature of our relations with the divinity or with the environment that surrounds us, whether biological or social. Are we truly free, or is our freedom conditional? Is it divine grace, or is it an act in which the mystery of the human person is revealed? These questions and others of their kind lead us to situate our freedom in the world. Freedom is not an ideal for abandoning the world but, rather, for making the world habitable. The opposite of Hindu liberation, whose ideal is the Absolute, the unconditional, my freedom has a limit, a condition: the freedom of others. Otherwise my freedom would be a form of despotism.

By the very nature of its suppositions, Indian tradition cannot conceive of freedom as a political ideal or incorporate it into the fabric of society. Not only is such freedom incompatible with the caste system, but India lacks a tradition of thinking critically. In its most genuine and most rigorous form, criticism can flourish only in a society that conceives of freedom as a good to be shared by all citizens. The relation between criticism of the gods and the right to vote and choose one's leaders has been evident since the time of Athenian democracy. Because they had democracy, the Greeks had tragedy, comedy, and free-thinking philosophy. In China, although there was political criticism, people never discussed the foundations of society as they did in Greece. Only in two periods of profound social crisis did the philosophical and political debate refer to original principles: in the era of the Warring States, and in the third century, when the Taoist philosophy of action-nonaction prevailed. In general, the criticism limited itself to praising or censuring the acts of the ministers of the Son of Heaven. The Chinese never doubted their institutions: they were defenders of a social order that for them was a reflection of the heavenly order. For Marx, the criticism of heaven was the beginning of a criticism of this world. He was not mistaken. Both criticisms are inseparable in a democracy.

Moksha means unconditional and absolute freedom. The liberated possesses limitless power over himself and over the reality that surrounds him: he has attained a superhuman state. He lives beyond passion and compassion, good and evil. He is as impassive and indifferent as the elements. India has always venerated the sannyāsi, who renounces ordinary existence for a life of asceticism and meditation. But a sannyāsi is not a redeemer, nor does he want to save the world: he knows that the world is already condemned. The world is māyā and duhkha: illusion and misery. It is time, the realm of the impermanent. Therefore, if the world is beyond help, and no one can save his neighbor, liberation can only be a project for hermits. The liberated is neither Christ nor Prometheus. Yet, as I said earlier, there is an exception: the doctrine that Krishna expounds to Arjuna in the *Bhagavad-Gītā*.

The origins of Krishna are obscure. He is the eighth avatar of Vishnu, but earlier he was a non-Aryan tribal god. Perhaps he was a cultural hero in archaic India. He is somewhat similar to Hercules in prowess, but also like Eros in his loves. He is a celestial deity: blue and black as the firmament.* The *Bhagavad-Gītā* is a religious and philosophical poem, inserted in the great epic the *Mahābhārata,* which takes the form of a dialogue between the hero Arjuna and the god Krishna, who appears as the driver of Arjuna's war chariot.

Before the battle begins, Arjuna wavers, consumed by remorse and foreboding. His dharma of the warring prince has brought him to combat, and moreover his cause is just; but the enemies he faces are of his blood: they are his cousins. To kill them would be an inexpiable crime against the laws of caste. Krishna dissuades him with these startling words: "You cry for those for whom you need not cry. The wise man weeps neither for the dead nor for the living." He then expounds the traditional doctrine of the unreality of the world. It is not a chimerical game but nature itself (*prakriti*) that leads man to act. He who thinks that he will kill in battle and he who thinks that he will be killed are both ignorant. The self is neither born nor does it die, it is indestructible and permanent: How can it kill or be killed? But if you nevertheless believe that your adversary can die, do not be afflicted

---

* I am indebted here to an interesting study by a young Mexican scholar, Benjamín Preciado: *The Krishna Cycle in the Purānas,* Delhi, 1984.

by it; to die is inevitable. All beings are born, die, and are reborn, but the self that inhabits every body is immortal and immutable. Arjuna replies, perplexed: "You say that the yoga of knowledge [the solitary path of meditation that leads to liberation] is superior to action. But now you say that action is illusory. So why do you impel me to commit these terrible deeds?" The god responds: "There is a twofold path: the yoga of knowledge and the yoga of action (karma yoga). Man is not liberated only through renunciation. Action also liberates." Krishna then further instructs Arjuna in the doctrine.

Until this point Krishna has limited himself to affirming that action is inevitable: to be born and to live is to work and to act. But how can action be legitimate, how can it be a path toward liberation? Krishna is a manifestation of Vishnu, the supreme god who creates the world, preserves and destroys it. Krishna continues: "There is nothing left in the three worlds for me to complete or to obtain; nevertheless I participate in action.... The worlds would be destroyed if I did not do my part. Therefore, as the ignorant man works out of an attachment to the act (or to himself), the wise man (like myself) works out of detachment and with the sole aim of helping the world." Philanthropy? Not entirely: Krishna speaks here in his aspect as a god who preserves the world. But it is one thing to preserve it, to keep it from falling into chaos and disorder, and another to change or redeem it: Krishna does proposes not the redemption but the preservation of the universal order. His purpose is to reveal to Arjuna the way that an act, regardless of its merit, has consequences and produces karma. He continues: "Although we are enchained by our acts and their consequences, there are certain actions that liberate us: those that we perform with absolute detachment." Krishna exhorts the hero to fulfill his duty as a warrior even if he causes suffering and innumerable deaths, on the condition that the action be undertaken and brought to an end in a state of disinterest. Krishna's doctrine is that of nonaction action, that is, an act that does not enchain the one who performs it.

It is impossible not to be moved by Krishna's teaching, and yet I wonder: Who could perform an act such as that? How and where could it be done? The hero of the *Bhagavad-Gītā* is doubly heroic: he is a warrior and a saint, a man of action and a quietist philosopher. The action that Krishna preaches could only be completed through a spiritual operation similar to that of the liberation of the solitary ascetic: by a total rupture of all the ties that bind us to the world, and by the destruction of the ego and of the illusion of time. We may imagine that moment: Arjuna sees Arjuna in combat and knows that he is and is not Arjuna; the true Arjuna is neither the combatant nor he who is watching the combat, but another, who has no name and who only *is*. In that same instant, the future vanishes and time dissolves: Arjuna becomes free of Arjuna. Who performs the act, and when? Everything happens in an eternal now, without antecedents or consequences, with no yesterday or tomorrow. Action without action is identical to liberation, and thus Krishna postulates a yoga of action to accompany the yoga of knowledge. The act executed by Arjuna: is it an act, or has it also vanished, along with the hero and his victims?

Krishna's doctrine is profound and sublime, but I would like tentatively to offer three observations. First: Between solitary liberation and the action that fatally engenders karma, Krishna does not really propose a new solution. Instead, he creates a bridge: there are actions that, if they are undertaken with true detachment, are equivalent to the act of the ascetic who detaches himself from his feelings and thoughts to reach the Absolute. In each case there is a rupture with the world, the death of the ego, and rebirth in a place where there is no night or day. Is it a reconciliation between action and quietude? I would say it is a transformation of action into a kind of dizzying quietude. The second observation: Although action does not enchain the hero, it does affect the others, all the men who will perish under his arrows and sword. Some, like Drona, are his teachers; others are his relatives, like his uncle Bhīshma. And what about their widows, children, parents, siblings, friends? The superhuman disinterest that Krishna preaches has another face: the indifference to the suffering of others. It is not simple—Arjuna's anguish proves it—to close one's eyes to the terrible consequences of the massacre. Thomas Aquinas's answer seems clearer: It is a sin to kill, but there are just wars. The third observation is a continuation of the second: The detachment of Arjuna is a personal act, a renunciation of himself and of his appetites, an act of spiritual heroism, yet one that does not reveal a love of one's neighbor. Arjuna saves no one except himself. Do I exaggerate? I don't think so: the least we can say is that Krishna preaches a disinterest without philanthropy. He teaches Arjuna how to escape karma and save himself, not how to save the others.

Here I end these reflections. It is not possible to define Indian civilization (including the Muslims, who also possess a beautiful mystic tradition) only, as is the custom in the West, through its religious and ascetic side. Gandhi was a true hero and a saint, but neither sanctity nor chastity define India. The apsarā and the yakshi even the balance: physical beauty also possesses a force that is, in its way, a spiritual magnetism. The Indian people are neither resigned nor ascetic. They have often been violent, and sensuality is a prominent feature in their art and customs. Passivity and asceticism are one side of the coin. Passivity is also a form of active love; asceticism is, in itself, eroticism and often violence: Krishna, Shiva, Durga are gods in love and in combat. The Indian genius is a love for abstraction and, at the same time, a passion for the concrete image. At times it is rich, at others, prolix. It fascinates us and tires us. It has created the most lucid and the most instinctive art. It is abstract and realistic, sexual and intellectual, pedantic and sublime. It lives between extremes, it embraces the extremes, rooted in the earth and drawn to an invisible beyond. On the one hand, a repetition of forms, a superimposition of concepts, a syncretism. On the other, the desire for totality and unity. And in its highest moments: the incarnation of a totality that is plenitude and emptiness, the transfiguration of the body into form that, without abandoning sensation and the flesh, is spiritual.

THE CONTRAPTIONS OF TIME

Every civilization is a vision of time. Institutions, works of art, technologies, philosophies, all that we make or dream is a weave of time. An idea or a sense of passage, time is not mere succession; for all cultures it is a process that has a direction, or points toward an end. Time has a meaning. Or, more precisely: time is the meaning of existence, even if we believe that existence has no meaning. The opposing attitudes of Hindus and Christians toward the human condition— karma and Original Sin, moksha and redemption—are also apparent in their different visions of time. Both are the manifestations and consequences of temporal succession: they not only exist in time and are made of time, but they are also an effect of an event that determines time and its direction. That event, in the case of Christianity, occurred before the beginning of time: Adam and Eve committed their sin in a place that previously was immune to change: Paradise. The story of humanity begins with the expulsion from Eden and our fall into history. In the case of Hinduism (and Buddhism), the cause is not anterior to, but rather inherent in time itself. In Christianity, time is the child of Original Sin, and thus its vision of time is negative, although not entirely so: man, through the sacrifice of Christ and through the exercise of his freedom, which is a gift of God, is capable of saving himself. Time is not only a life sentence, it is also a test. For the Hindu, time in itself is evil. By its very nature impermanent and changing, it is illusory. It is time, it is māyā: a lie with a charming appearance that is nothing but suffering, error, and finally the death that condemns us to be reborn in the horrible fiction of another life that is equally painful and unreal.

For Christians, Jews, and Muslims, there was only one creation. In Hinduism, Louis Renau notes, "classical cosmography imagined an egg of Brahma out of which came a series of successive creations."* It is not one creation but many. Renau adds: "The duration of the universe, from its beginning to its dissolution, is one day for Brahma; an infinity of births precede it, and other dissolutions will follow it." The universe lasts as long as Brahma sleeps and dreams. When he wakes, the universe will vanish, but it will be born anew when the god goes back to sleep. Brahma is condemned to dream the world, and we are condemned to be his dream. We know the duration of these recurrent dreams: 2,190,000

---

* Louis Renau, *La civilisation de l'Inde ancienne d'après les textes sanscrites.* Paris, 1950.

terrestrial years. (In other versions it is 4,320,000 years.) Every cycle (*kalpa*) is composed of four ages (*yugas*). In the current kalpa, we are now living in the fourth and last of these ages, the *Kali yuga*. It is the age of error, the mixing of the castes, and the degradation of the social and cosmic order. Its end is approaching, and all will be destroyed by fire and water. After a period of cosmic lethargy, the universe will begin another cycle. Thus time can stop, it has an end; but it is reborn and runs through the same cycle; it is an infinity.* In Buddhism and Jainism there are similar cycles and numbers. Compare the vastness of these cycles with the Christian assumption of the age of the world: a few thousand years. And in Hindu, Buddhist, and Jain cosmology—as well as in Giordano Bruno and many modern scientific hypotheses—there is also a plurality of worlds inhabited by intelligent creatures. In each one of these worlds there are other Buddhas and Mahaviras. (Mahavira was the founder of Jainism.) The Buddhist texts even tell us that there is a future Buddha who, when mankind has forgotten, will teach us again the way to nirvāna. We already know his name: Maitreya.

The idea of successive cosmic creations with corresponding world ages appears in many cultures. It was a belief among the American Indians; the ancient Mexicans said that there were five creations, which they called "suns." The fifth and final age is the current one: the "sun of movement." These beliefs appear in other cultures in the Orient, in Asia Minor, and the Mediterranean, and they were shared by various philosophers: Pythagoras, Empedocles, Plato, the Stoics. Another similarity between Hindus and the Greco-Romans: the idea

---

* See Luis González Reiman, *Tiempo cíclico y eras del mundo en la India,* El Colegio de México, 1988.

that the sublunar world is imperfect because it ceaselessly changes. Change is the sign of a deficiency. Man, the incomplete being, aspires to the plenitude of Being, which is identical to his Self. Change, the incessant mutations of time and the world, aspires to the immutable identity of Being. For the Greeks and the Hindus, movement was difficult to understand, except as the attempt to reach the immutability of Being that is beyond time. Heraclitus conceived of the world not as a progression based on a struggle between opposites—which is the modern interpretation of his beliefs, one which I think is mistaken—but as a rhythm composed of successive ruptures followed by reconciliations: the one divides into two halves that hate each other, then love each other and reunite, only to separate again . . . and so on, until the end of time. Not "elective affinities" but affinities ruled by fate: every affirmation engenders its negation, which in turn is negated and becomes an affirmation. Heraclitus did not know progress. Neither did Plato or Aristotle, who saw the circle as the image of perfection: the beginning is also the end. The circle is the image of the eternal motion of celestial bodies. Movement longs for immobility, time for immutability.

The complexity of Hindu cosmography and the enormous duration of its cycles seem to belong to the logic that rules nightmares. In the end, these cosmographies vanish: we open our eyes and realize that we have lived among phantasms. The dream of Brahma, what we call reality, is a mirage, a nightmare. To wake is to discover the unreality of this world. The negative character of time is not the consequence of Original Sin but of its opposite: man's Original Sin or fault is to be the child of time. The evil is in time itself. Why is time evil? Because it lacks substance: it is a dream, a lie, māyā. The word is usually translated as "illusion," but one must add that the illusion that is the world is a divine creation. One of the Upanishads says: "You must know that Nature (prakriti) is illusion (māyā) and that the Lord is a creator of illusions (*mayin*)." In the *Bhagavad-Gītā,* explaining to Arjuna about his births, Krishna says: "Although I was not born and my being is immortal . . . I was incarnated in a mortal being in this world through my power (māyā)." Here māyā is power. But, Krishna adds in another passage, "those who seek refuge in me, pierce through that divine power (māyā)." Thus māyā is equally illusion and the power to create appearances. The one true reality is neither creation nor appearance: it is immutable and uncreated Being. For the Buddhist, it is emptiness. Māyā is time, not in the Western sense—a dynamic process—but the useless repetition of a false reality, an apparition. Everything that changes suffers from unreality; the real is what lasts: Absolute Being (Brahman). Man is as impermanent as the cosmos, but at his depths is the Self (ātman) that is identical to the universal Self. Both are beyond time, beyond happening. The Self neither thinks nor feels nor changes: it is. Buddhism, in turn, denies the Self and sees the ego as a conjunction of insubstantial elements which meditation must disperse and then dissolve. Hinduism and Buddhism are radical critiques of time.

For Hinduism, time has no meaning, or, more exactly, it has no meaning other than its obliteration by total Being, as Krishna tells Arjuna. This conception of time explains the absence of a historical consciousness among Hindus. India has had great poets, philosophers, architects, and painters, but it has never, until modern times, had a great historian. Among the various means of negating time among the Hindus, there are two that are particularly astonishing: metaphysical negation and social negation. The first prevented the birth of that literary, scientific, and philosophical genre we call history. The second, the institution of the castes, immobilized society.

The contrast with the Muslims and the Chinese is remarkable. For the Chinese, perfection was in the past. Confucius remarked: "I do not invent, I transmit. I believe in Antiquity and I love it." Civilization is an order that is no different from the natural and cosmic order: it is a rhythm. Barbarianism is the transgression of the rules of nature, the confusion of the heavenly principle with the earthly, the mixing of the five elements and the four points of the horizon: a rupture of the cosmic rhythm. Barbarianism is not anterior to history; it is outside of it. The dawn of civilization, the mythic happy age of the Yellow Emperor, is also its noon, its highest moment. The apogee is at the birth, the beginning is perfection and therefore the archetype for excellence. Antiquity is perfect because it represents the state of harmony between the natural world and the social world. Thus the importance of the five Classic Books: They are the source of political knowledge and the foundation of the art of government; politics is one part of the theory of universal correspondence; music, poetry, dance, and the rites are political because they are rhythm; the imitation of the ancients is the path to knowledge and virtuous government. The Taoist heterodoxy did not believe in the classics or in civilization or in virtue, in the sense given these words by Confucius and his disciples, but agreed with them in seeing nature as a model: wisdom is in accord with the rhythm of nature, knowledge is not a knowing, but a tuning of the soul. The meaning of time is in the past; Antiquity is the sun that illuminates our works, judges our acts, guides our steps.

Among the Muslims, history is a chronicle, not a meditation on time. Ibn Khaldun, however, divides human societies into two groups: primitive cultures and civilizations. The former, whether nomadic or sedentary, do not properly understand history: tied to the earth or wandering in the desert, they live permanently in the same time. Civilizations are born, reach their apogee, decline and disappear: goats come to graze around their ruined stones. Civilizations are individual organisms, each one with its own characteristics, but all are subject to the laws of birth and death. And yet they contain a timeless element: religion. True perfection is not in time but in religions—above all, in the ultimate religion, Islam, which is the definitive revelation.

Christian time is linear rather than cyclical. It has a beginning (Adam and Eve and the Fall), an intermediate point (the sacrifice and redemption of Christ), and a final period (ours). Christian time breaks the circular rhythm of paganism. For Plato and Aristotle, the perfect movement is circular: the image of the heavenly bodies, it is rational and eternal. Linear time is accidental and finite; it is contingent: it moves not by itself, but due to the impulse of an outside agent. Christianity inverts the terms: human, linear time is what matters, because it leads to our salvation or damnation. It is neither eternal nor indefinite movement; it has an end, in both senses of the word: termination and goal. Because of the first, it is definite; because of the second, it has a meaning; because of both, it is decisive. Christianity introduces decision and freedom: its time implies redemption or perdition. Merit does not reside in the past, although the Fall was the cause of time and of history, but in the present: right now I can save or damn myself. And this now belongs to a future that is also defined: the final hour, whether the death of the individual or the Final Judgment. Christianity coincides with the other religions in conceiving of perfection as something beyond time, but its beyond is neither in the past nor outside of time; it is in a precise and definite future: the end of time. That end is the beginning of something that is not time, something that we cannot name, although we sometimes call it eternity.

The modern concept of time is based on that of Christianity. Time for us is linear succession, history—not sacred, but profane. The conversion of sacred time into profane time had the immediate consequence of transforming it: time ceased to be finite and defined, and became infinite and indefinite. Modern time is a permanent beyond, a future that is forever unreachable and unrealizable. That future is indefinable because it has no end or goal: its essence is untouchable. And as the future drifts farther away, so does the past; it too is untouchable. Yet we can explore it and calculate with some precision the antiquity of the human species, and even that of the earth and the solar system. In contrast, the future is and will be incalculable. Perhaps someday we will know where we came from, but it is unlikely that we'll ever know where we're going. An arrow shot forward, moving in a straight line, our time has no more meaning than that of a being in perpetual motion, getting closer to—getting farther from—the future perfection. The idea that spurs us on is marvelous and meaningless: the future is progress.

The European expansion disrupted the rhythm of the Eastern societies: it shattered the shape of time and the meaning of its passage. It was more than an invasion. Those peoples had suffered other dominations and knew what it was like to be under a foreign yoke, but the European presence seemed to them to be a *dissonance*. Some tried to find a purpose to all that frenetic activity, to that will that extended toward an indefinite future. Upon discovering what this idea was based on, they were scandalized: to think that time is endless progress, not a mystical paradox, seemed to them an aberration. But there was also wonder in their distress: no matter how irrational the concept, it was also clear that it had led the Europeans to create marvels. The contempt that the Hindu and Muslim elites had for Western materialism was quickly transformed into admiration. They realized that, although the English were no wiser than themselves, they were far more powerful. Their knowledge did not lead one to the contemplation of divinity or to liberation; their science was action: nature obeyed them, and in their cities the power of the rich and strong was less oppressive. The old magic was now in reach of everyone who knew the formula for the spell.

Science and technology, our power over the material world and the freedom that power gives us: this is the secret of the fascination the West held for the elites of the ancient East. It was a true vertigo: time mattered less, men were not the slaves of either the revolutions of the stars or of karmic law. The moment could take the form that our knowledge and our will imposed upon it. The world had become malleable. The appearance of modern time resulted in an inversion of traditional values, in Europe as well as in Asia: the rupture of the pagan cyclical time, the destruction of Hindu absolute timelessness, the discrediting of the Chinese past, the end of the Christian eternity. A dispersion and multiplication of perfection: its house is the future, and the future is everywhere and nowhere, within hand's reach and always ungraspable. Progress ceased to be an idea and became a faith. It changed the world and changed souls. It did not redeem us from our contingency: it exalted it as an adventure that was always beginning anew. Man was no longer a creature of time but its creator.

The traps of time: precisely in the moment when the idolatry of change, the belief in progress as a historical law, and the preeminence of the future have triumphed all over the world, these ideas have begun to crumble. Two world wars and the establishment of totalitarian tyrannies have shaken our faith in progress; technological civilization has shown that it possesses immense powers of destruction, for the natural world as well as for the cultural and spiritual environment. Poisoned rivers, forests turned to wastelands, contaminated cities, uninhabited souls. The civilization of abundance is also that of famines in Africa and other places. The collapse of Nazism and totalitarian Communism has left intact all the evils of the democratic liberal societies, ruled by the demon of money. Marx's famous phrase about religion as the opiate of the masses can now be applied, and more accurately, to television, which will end up anaesthetizing the human race, sunk in an idiotic beatitude. The future has ceased to be a radiant promise and has become a grim question.

For Gandhi, civilizations came and went, the only thing that remained standing was dharma: the truth of the humble with no other sword than that of nonviolence. In a certain sense, he was correct: history is the great constructor of ruins. Opposed to the dangerous inventions of the West, he kept his faith in a society composed of small villages of farmers and artisans. History itself, in its blindest and most brutal form, has proven him wrong: the population explosion has smashed the dream of happy villages. Every village is a pit of misery and despair. We all know it, but most of us don't know it well enough: our idea of time has cracked apart, and its miraculous inventions have burned our hands and minds. Perhaps the answer is to place at the center of the triad of time, between the past that drifts off and the future that we'll never reach, the present. The concrete reality of every day. I believe that the reformation of our civilization must begin with a reflection on time. A new politics must be based on the present. But that is another subject, and one that I have dealt with elsewhere.... These pages began with an attempt to answer a question I had in India. Now I end with a question that concerns us all: In what time do we live?

Farewell

The final year of my stay in India coincided with the great youth rebellions. I followed them, from afar, with astonishment and with hope. I did not understand clearly the meaning of these movements; but, it could be said in my favor, neither did their protagonists. What we did know was that they were a rebellion against the values and ideas of modern society. The demonstrations were instigated not by the old left but by a libertarian spirit, and for this alone it was admirable. The student rebellion in Paris in 1968 was the most inspired, and the one that made the greatest impression on me. The words and acts of those young people seemed to me the legacy of some of the great modern poets who were both rebels and prophets: Blake, Hugo, Whitman. As I was thinking about these things, the summer of 1968 brought them close to home. The excessive heat had led Marie José and me to seek temporary refuge in a village in the foothills of the Himalayas, an old summer retreat for the British called Kasauli. We set ourselves up in a small hotel, the only one in the village, still managed by two elderly English ladies, survivors of the Raj. I had taken along a shortwave radio that allowed me to listen every day to the news and commentary from the BBC in London.

We walked in the countryside around Kasauli, but neither the views of the enormous mountains and the Indian plains below, nor the enchanting gardens full of hydrangeas—English gardening at the foot of sublime peaks—could keep us from the events in Paris. In those weeks I felt that the hopes of my own youth had been reborn: if the workers and the students could unite, we would be witnessing the first true socialist revolution. Perhaps Marx had not been wrong: the revolution would explode in an advanced country, with an established proletariat educated in democratic traditions. That revolution would spread throughout the developed world, and would mark the end of capitalism and of the totalitarian regimes that had usurped the name of socialism in Russia, China, Cuba, and other places. And something new, which was not foreseen by Marx: that revolution would also be the beginning of a profound change of consciousness. Poetry, heir of the great spiritual traditions of the West, had become action. It was the realization of the dreams of the Romantics in the nineteenth century and of the Surrealists in the twentieth. I had never been completely convinced by the poetics and aesthetics of Surrealism. I practiced "automatic writing" only a few times, and I have always believed that poetry somehow inextricably combines both inspiration and calculation. What attracted me to Surrealism, above all, was its union of poetry and action. This is, for me, the essence or the meaning of the word "revolution." André Breton had died barely two years before, precisely at the moment when these ideas, which he had embodied in admirable and exemplary manner, began to gather strength and historical reality.

Events soon disillusioned me. We were witnessing, yes, a sort of tremor, not of the earth but of consciousness. The explanation of the phenomenon was not in Marxism but rather, perhaps, in the history of religions, in the psychic sub-soil of Western civilization. A sick civilization: the student demonstrations were like those fevers that quickly pass but are the symptoms of something far more serious. We returned to Delhi, and there more news was waiting for me: in Mexico City, too, the students were rebelling. It was largely an echo of what had already happened in the United States, Germany, and France. The rebellion was limited to Mexico City and generally confined to more or less affluent middle-class youth. It was not a proletariat movement, nor did it attempt to attract the workers. But it had put the government in a difficult position: at that moment it was preparing to host the Olympic Games in Mexico City a few months later. What happened in Mexico, moreover, had certain unique characteristics and was not a mere reflection of the events that had shaken other countries. The Mexican movement lacked the moral, social, and sexual critique of bourgeois society, and the poetic and orgiastic anarchism of the Parisian rebels, expressed in such electric phrases as "It is prohibited to prohibit" or "The beach is under the pavement"—lines that recalled the Surrealist manifestoes and declarations of forty years before. In contrast, many of the demands of the Mexican youths were quite con-crete; among them, one that was and still is the heart of po-litical polemic in Mexico: democracy.

The demand for a democratic reform of the government was an aspiration shared by much of the country, particularly the expanding middle class. Mexicans were tired of the continual domination by the official party (the Institutional

Revolutionary Party, or PRI), which had survived since the historical and political necessities that had given it birth in 1929. Of course, the true purpose of the student leaders was of a revolutionary nature: they saw democracy only as a base from which to leap to the second stage, in which socialism would be established. In this, their ideology was radically different from that of the rebels in Paris. The Mexican youths were magnetized by the example of Che Guevara. A model, I would say in passing, that was both suicidal and useless: history had already taken another course from that of Che. But the conjunction of the student rebellion and the word "democracy" had become immensely popular among the students in Mexico City.

At that moment, I received a communication from the Mexican Secretary of Foreign Relations, Antonio Carrillo Flores, an affable, intelligent, sensible man. He asked me to inform him what measures the Indian government had taken in situations like those in Mexico. It was a letter similar to one sent to all the ambassadors. In my response, besides sending the information he requested, I added a long personal note. My essential argument, somewhat amplified, was published later as *Postdata* (*Postscript,* 1969).* I attempted to justify the positions of the students, insofar as they were concerned with democratic reform. Above all, I recommended that force not be used and that a political solution be found to the conflict. Carrillo Flores answered me with a telegram: he thanked me for my response, had read my commentary with great attention, and had shown it to the President, who had expressed

---

* Published in English as part of *The Other Mexico: Critique of the Pyramid,* Grove Press, New York, 1972.

equal interest. I slept easily for the next ten or twelve days, until, on the morning of October 3, I learned of the bloody repression of the previous day. I decided that I could no longer represent a government that was operating in a manner so clearly opposite to my way of thinking. I wrote to Carrillo Flores to communicate my decision, and visited the Indian Minister of Foreign Affairs to inform him.

The reaction of the Indian government was extremely friendly and discreet. Indira Gandhi, who was then Prime Minister, could not officially see me off, but she invited Marie José and me to a small dinner at her house, with Rajiv, his wife, Sonia, and a few mutual friends. The writers and artists organized a sort of farewell tribute at the International House. There were articles and interviews in the press. The correspondent from *Le Monde,* Jean Wetz, a good friend, published an extensive commentary on the case. A few days later, we took the train to Bombay, where we were to board the *Victoria,* a steamship that traveled from Asia to the Mediterranean. The trip from Delhi to Bombay was emotional, not only because I remembered the one I had made nearly twenty years before, but also because along the way, at various stations, groups of students would board the train to offer us the traditional garlands of flowers. In Bombay we stayed at the Taj Mahal and visited some friends. We spent the last Sunday on the island of Elephanta. It had been my first experience of Indian art; it had also been the first for Marie José, years after mine though before we had met. There were many tourists, which at first ruined our visit. But the beauty of the place conquered all the distractions and intrusions. The blue of the sea and the sky; the curving bay and its banks, some white, others green, ocher, violet; the island fallen in the water like an enormous stone; the cave and, in the half-light, the sculptures, images of beings that are of this world and of another that we can only glimpse . . . I relived what we had felt years ago, but now illumined by another, more serious light: we thought that we were seeing all this for the last time. It was as though we were leaving ourselves. Time opened its doors: What was waiting for us? That night, returning to the hotel, as an invocation and as a way of saying good-bye, I wrote these lines:

> Shiva and Pārvatī:
> > we worship you
> not as gods
> > but as images
> of the divinity of man.
> You are what man makes and is not,
> what man will be
> when he has served the sentence of hard labor.
> Shiva:
> > your four arms are four rivers,
> four jets of water.
> > > Your whole being is a fountain
> where the lovely Pārvatī bathes,
> where she rocks like a graceful boat.
> The sea beats beneath the sun:
> it is the great lips of Shiva laughing;
> the sea is ablaze:
> it is the steps of Pārvatī on the waters.
> Shiva and Pārvatī:
> > > the woman who is my wife
> and I
> > ask you for nothing, nothing

that comes from the other world:

only

the light on the sea,

the barefoot light on the sleeping land and sea.

Mexico City, 20 December 1994

ACKNOWLEDGMENTS

This book does not end with a bibliography. It would be pointless: this is not a systematic study, but a more or less ordered gathering of the reflections, impressions, and objections that India provoked in me. The landscapes, monuments, music, dance and, above all, the people marked me more deeply than any reading. Of course, it is impossible to mention everything I saw and lived, the people with whom I spoke and to whom I listened, the Ganges and the deserts of Rajasthan, the sea in Bengal and Kerala, Oootacamund and the temples of Orissa, a cabdriver in Calcutta or the saddhu in Galta, the Brahmans of Chindambaram or the Parsi millionaire in Bombay, the Catholic priest in Cochin, the poets and dancers in Delhi, the two elderly English ladies who ruled the little hotel in Kausali. Nevertheless, it would be ungracious not to mention at least a few of the friends who accompanied and guided Marie José and me in those years.

My first friends, in 1952, were the writer Krishna Kripallani and his wife, a granddaughter of Tagore. They initiated me in modern Hindi and Bengali literature. Thanks to them—or was it to Henri Michaux?—I met Lokenath Bhattacharya, the author of short stories and texts that, in a simple style, attempt to evoke the least tangible reality: absence. Narayan Menon, a notable musicologist and lover of poetry, introduced me, with tact, patience, and wisdom, to two subtle and complex arts: Indian music and dance. Finally, I had the good fortune to help a talented young painter, Satish Gujrat, receive a fellowship to travel to Mexico.

This circle of friends widened during my second stay (1962–68). The first I should mention is J. Swaminathan, a close friend who is now gone. A painter and poet, he was a spirit who united an originality of vision with an intellectual rigor. The brilliant Sham Lal, who was as deeply read in modern Western thought as he was in the philosophical traditions of India, particularly Buddhism. Krisnan Khannan, a painter of solid and balanced volume. The political essayist Romesh Thapar, a man of great vitality and intellectual perspicacity; his wife, Raj, who was no less sharp and lively; his sister, the well-known historian Romila Thapar. The novelist Ruth Prawer Jhabvala, known not only for her intelligent screen adaptations of various novels by E. M. Forster, but for her own work as well. Kushwant Singh, a restless journalist and author of a two-volume history of the Sikhs. The painter Hussain, the oldest and youngest of the Indian painters, with one foot in the avant-garde and the other in tradition. Two notable poets, Agyeya (S. Vatsyanan), the patriarch of Hindi poetry, and Shikrant Verma, a young man who died too soon.

I had many conversations with the novelist Mulk Raj Anand on a subject that fascinated us both: the Tantric tradition. We had musician friends, such as Chatur Lal, a master of the *tabla* who drank whiskey like a Scot. More painters: Gaytonde, whose abstract landscapes, bearing no relation to reality, were nonetheless Bombay sunsets; J. Kumar, a smiling man and an artist of severe constructions; Ambadas, who now lives in Norway. And two notable women: Pupul Jayakar, the well-known author of various beautiful books that are indispensable for a knowledge of Indian folk art, and Usha Bhagat, an expert on the folk music of the north.

It is impossible not to recall a Catalan Hindu, both a theologian and a migratory bird in all climates from Benares to Santa Barbara, California: Raimundo Panikkar. A man of electric intelligence, with whom I would spend hours discussing some controversial point in the *Gita* or a Buddhist sutra—I have never heard anyone attack the heresy of Buddhism with such furious dialectics as Panikkar.

Finally, another conversationalist with razor-sharp logic: Nirad C. Chaudhuri. A gnome, a little elf who would immediately capture our attention with his witticisms, his irreverent reflections, his arbitrary opinions, his culture and his sarcasm, his valiant, insolent sincerity. Chaudhuri is the author of a masterpiece, *The Autobiography of an Unknown Indian,* and of various books of caustic and penetrating essays on his country and fellow countrymen. His last book, *Thy Hand, Great Anarch! India, 1921–1952,* a volume of more than nine hundred pages, is perhaps too prolix for a foreigner who is not interested in all the details of Indian politics, but it contains remarkable passages that illuminate the history of modern India with another light, crueler but more real. The last chapter, "Credo et Intelligam," is a philosophical and moral testament that is both moving and makes us think.